Justice for Baby Josh

Written by R. Granville Coleman
Co-authored by Jordan Leigh Kahill

i

In Memory of

Josh Cade Hinson

May 10, 1995- October 20, 1996

Conceived in deceit, born for profit,

who, in the 17 months of his so short life,

never felt a mother's love,

his father's hand,

or knew his grandmother's grief.

This book is dedicated to:

Tabor City Police officers Jerome Russell and Robert Moyer, who twice tried to save Brittany and Josh.
Tabor City volunteer firemen Tracey and Jeff Fowler, who risked their lives to carry Brittany, and Josh, from their fiery bedrooms.
Tabor City volunteer Fire Chief Jerry Watts, for bringing order to the chaos of that 4:00 AM holocaust.
Tabor City Volunteer Firemen
Buddy Wally, Gary Watts, et al.
Tabor City Ambulance driver Gary Sikes, who rushed Brittany to the Loris, SC Hospital in time to save her life.
Tabor Rescue Squad members Melissa Sikes and Lorrie Lancaster, whose tears and prayers mothered Brittany's rush to the hospital.
Tabor City police officer Annie Gause, whose woman's presence during those fateful minutes was priceless.
Tabor City fireman/ambulance driver Gary Watts and rescue workers Ronnie and Sondra Watts, who desperately tried to save baby Josh's life.
Dana Hammond and Betty Gore, whose courage to come forward, despite threats against their lives, gave hope for justice for Josh in death, denied him in life.

Justice for Baby Josh

More Book from Uncommon Sense Publishing

My One Night Stand with God's Assassin –

Jocelyn Otis-Coleman

The Governor's Fingerprints – R. G. Coleman, Ph.D

Trump's Troupes Revolt Against Republican Party's

Betrayal - R. G. Coleman, P.h.D.

Alice's Wonderland – R. G. Coleman, P.h.D.

Good Dad, Bad Mom, Part I – R. G. Coleman, P.h.D

Good Dad, Bad Mom, Part II – R. G. Coleman, P.h.D.

"911--Is this an emergency?" the female dispatcher asks.

"911! Help!" a woman screams a hard, dry scream.

-- "What's the problem?"

"My house is on FIRE!"

"Your house is on fire?"

"YES!"

"Ok. Hang on ma'am. Hang on. Are you at your house now?"

"YES! My kids are upstairs and I can't get them!"

-- "You cannot get them?"

"My house is engulfed in flames --"

"I'm paging at this time. Are you able to get the children out --"

"I can't even get upstairs!"

"Hang on just a second --"

"Help please!"

"Tabor City Fire Department -- I need you to respond -- 101 South Wall Street -- Be advised house engulfed in flames --"

"Help me!"

"-- Be advised subjects trapped inside --"

"MA'AM!"

"-- 2-33 traffic. 10-33 traffic -- time 03:57 --"

"MA'AM!"

"-- Calling Central -- clear -- You said there are kids upstairs?"

"Yes. Both bedrooms! Upstairs!"

"Ok, and you said the upstairs is engulfed in flames?"

"It's completely engulfed and I can't get up there -- It's just burnin'."

"Ok--"

"Please hurry! Things are falling... Oh, God! I'm goin' to lose my   young'uns!"

"Ok --Ok. The station is alerted. That means they're going to get there as fast as they can. We've also dispatched police -- We've got police coming too --"

"Help me--"

"We're going to get you as much help as you need --"

"Please!"

"Ok -- How many people are in the house?"

"Them two kids and me!"

"Just them two and you?"

"Oh, God! It's coming through the kitchen! It's coming through the kitchen! Oh, God, my young-uns are gone! My young-uns are gone! My babies are gone! Oh, they're gone! My babies are gone!"

(Aside) "Those people need to talk to a police officer."

"My babies are gone. I can't get them."

"Ok, the officer's there --"

"Help me! Help me! My babies! Help me! Please help my babies!"

"-- Calling Central Station -- Be advised subjects still trapped inside. They will be on the second floor! Two children --"

(To police officers at the scene) "-- Straight in ... both of them -- I can't get them, ya'll! Please hurry. They're my babies!"

"-- Central Station calling Tabor City Rescue -- respond to 101 South Wall Street -- repeat -- We need you to respond to 101 South Wall Street --"

"Oh, God! ... You need me anymore?"

"-- Be advised children will be trapped upstairs -- 10-33 traffic -- 03:59."

"--Can you help me?"

"-- 10-33 traffic--"

"MA'AM!"

"I'm still here. I'm still here. I'm paging Rescue Two --"

"Are you through with me? They're trying -- They can't get to them!"

"They can't get to them? I'm going to let you go -- If

2

they're there -- Do you see the police officers?"

"Yeh. I got to get out of here!"

"All right. Bye, bye."

As Officer Russell lurches from his patrol car to run to the house, the lights from Officer Moyer's on-rushing police car cuts through the cloud of silty sand caused by Russell's car. The two officers run toward the front door just as it opens, revealing the silhouette of a white female – mid-30's, wearing glasses, jeans, shirt, socks and shoes, holding a cordless phone in one hand and a cigarette case in the other. She points up the stairs, "Straight in -- both of them -- I can't get them, ya'll. Please hurry! They're my babies!"

Officer Moyer starts up the stairs, gets to within 4-5 steps of the top, begins coughing, can't breathe, turns, and retreats.

Russell runs outside. Moyer, still gasping, follows. They race around to the back in a desperate search for another entrance. Russell tries the side door, not realizing it will only get him into the kitchen. The door is locked. Pressing his face against the window, he sees a table up against the door.

The officers race back to the front. The woman is still talking on her cordless phone.

Officer Russell tries to go up the stairs, but before he too reaches the top, the smoke stings his face as if being attacked by a thousand bees. The only light which penetrates the suffocating smoke comes from the bright frightening orange flames under the closed bedroom door at the head of the stairs. No longer able to hold his breath, now beginning to feel as if his lungs were drowning, Russell flees this stairway to hell.

Officer Moyer, with his partner following behind, hustle the woman outside just as the first fire truck skids into the yard.

"The kids are upstairs!" Russell spits and sputters to the firemen.

Justice for Baby Josh

As they watch the fireman pull hose, the woman offers, "The electric heater caused the fire upstairs. That's why I slept downstairs -- We've had some problems with the downstairs radiator." (Officer Russell would later recall that the woman had no burns, nor did her hair appear to have been singed. In his report, Russell noted that when he answered the 911 call, gray smoke was pouring out of a hole in the roof. No flames, just smoke. The two upstairs dormer windows of this small two-story brick rental were black. The only light was from a solitary downstairs window just to the right of the front door.)

Volunteer fireman Tracey Fowler just got home this chilly October 20th night from fighting another house fire. Before he could crawl into bed, his pager sounds. "Tabor City Fire Department -- I need you to respond -- 101 South Wall St. Be advised house is engulfed in flames."

Fowler turns onto South Wall St. just a few blocks from downtown. It's about 4:00 A.M. One policeman is placing markers to block Wall Street. Fowler sees orange flames spewing into the October night from the center of the roof's back slope. The pumper is already there and firemen are pulling hoses.

Fowler jumps out of his truck and begins putting on his air pack.

An officer hurries over. "The young'uns are upstairs. The girl is to my left and the boy is upstairs straight ahead."

Fowler enters the house followed by Volunteer Fire Chief Jerry Watts carrying a flashlight. The single living room light is still on, but the rest of the house wears death's mourning black. (The firemen later reported having trouble locating and pulling the electric meter box.)

Chief Watts tells Fowler, "Go upstairs and get the young-uns."

As Fowler hurries up the stairs, he can't get his fire gloves on because they are still wet from the previous fire that night. By the time he reaches the top of the stairs, he still isn't able to get his gloves all the way on.

Chief Watts' trailing flashlight first loses Fowler from the waist up in the smoke, then all together, Fowler vanishes.

It's hot -- very hot, but Fowler doesn't see any fire -- as if he's entered a walk-in oven set at 1,000 degrees... he thinks he hears a little cry... dropping to his knees, he begins crawling toward the sound to his left, all the while frantically attempting to tug his gloves on. Like a blind man, he feels his way along the floor. He senses he's entering a room... his knees hit something -- he fumbles through the black -- he feels a leg -- a little leg -- then a head -- face down as if the child had been trying to escape underneath the bed.

Fowler throws off his gloves, grabs the child under its chest and legs, and like an amputee on his knees, stumbles out of the room. He stands and then listens, trying to pierce the crackling sound of the fire eating the house. Holding the child close to his ear, he hears no breathing from the limp and lifeless body in his arms.

Fowler hurries down the stairs. Outside, he looks down at the child -- a little girl – a blond-haired little girl of about four years. He hands her to a rescue squad member, turns away, and re-enters the house.

Fowler rushes back upstairs. Finding his way into the bedroom on the left, not knowing Tracey has just come from there, he finds neither child. He hears water being shot against the upstairs bedroom window at the head of the stairs, where he now enters. Again, he feels the tremendous heat, but no flames in sight. The smoke level is near the floor, so he drops to his knees and begins crawling. His face mask is leaking. He's breathing smoke. He sees the leg of a crib, jumps up, and reaches to grab the baby's body.

Outside the window, the fireman on the ladder sees Fowler's reflective gear and stops spraying the window.

Tracey Fowler had seen Jeff coming out of the

bedroom to the right. Thinking that the other child may be in the same room where he'd found the little girl, Tracey re-enters that room.

He hears Jeff call, "I've got him!"

Tracey's air pack alarm bell sounds. He grabs Jeff's straps, to keep him from tripping on the fire hose on the stairs. (Jeff would later estimate that from the time he entered the house until he got outside with the infant took about 4-5 minutes). Once outside, Jeff carries the charred body to the second rescue ambulance, trips on the hose in the yard, rolls on his side, dropping the baby.

Gary Watts of the rescue squad scoops up the baby, checks its pulse, and then rushes the baby into the ambulance.

(On Wednesday, or four days after the Sunday fire, Columbus County 911 notified Tracey Fowler that the mother, Terri Hinson, wanted him to call her. He did. She asked, "Where did you find my daughter, Brittany?"

He told her "on the floor in her room."

The mother started talking about the fire and all the damage that was done. Finally, the mother thanked Fowler but he wondered why the mother didn't seem upset recalling the event. To Tracey Fowler, she seemed nervous and talked very fast, but not sad or grieving. She didn't even mention that he saved her daughter's life.)

Corporal Annie Gause hears the 911 call on her portable radio in her car on her way home from work. She arrives at 101 South Wall Street, Officers Moyer and Russell is standing outside the house with the woman, later identified as Terri Hinson. The woman appears to be talking on the phone.

As Officer Gause approaches, the woman begins yelling, "Save my babies!"

The female officer does not see any burns on the woman, nor can she tell from the poor lighting in the yard if her hair is singed.

6

Officer Gause ushers the mother out of the way of the firefighters.

The two women back across the street, standing at the edge of the neighbor's driveway. Terri Hinson explains she had checked on the children several times and "closed the bedroom doors because it was so hot in their rooms."

Then, the mother says, "My little boy is dead."

When Tracy Fowler brings out Brittany, Officer Gause comments, "Ma'am, there's your little girl."

The mother answers, "Where's my little boy?" As the rescue workers place Brittany in the ambulance, Hinson adds, "I can't lose it -- I can't lose these. I've already lost three -- one's adopted in Kentucky, one's in Fair Bluff, and I don't know where the third one is. If I lose these, they will have to kill me!"

"Don't you want to ride in the ambulance?" Gause asks.

"I've called my boyfriend to come pick me up."

Gause crosses the street to where the rescue squad is trying to revive the little girl.

The mother heads toward the neighbor's house, yelling, "Get my children! Get my children out!"

The neighbor, later identified as officer Lewis of the State Highway Patrol, comes out of his house, says something to the woman, turns, then seeing his wife exit the back door, joins her as they approach the mother. The three begin walking toward the neighbor's back yard.

Fowler exits the burning house carrying Terri Hinson's 17-month old baby boy, Josh.

The mother who had been doing all the yelling, screaming, and pleading, never even moves toward either ambulance, never asks about her children, does not inquire as to which hospital her children will be taken, and even refuses to accompany either of her children in the ambulance. She tells the drivers, "I'm waiting for my boyfriend."

The Tabor City Rescue Squad had already worked a fatal fire earlier that night. An hour later, they responded to a "sick call" and as they were returning the ambulance, the driver, Gary Sikes comments. "I smell smoke." It was around 4:00 A.M. Within seconds, they were paged by 911 to 101 South Wall St.

Upon their arrival, a woman meets them in the road screaming, "You made me leave my babies." (Sikes would later recall, "The woman, later identified as the children's mother, Terri Hinson, is fully dressed in blue jeans, tennis shoes, a short-sleeved shirt, carrying a cordless telephone, cigarette case, and wearing glasses. Her hair appears to be singed slightly around the edges.")

The ambulance pulls in behind the Tabor City Fire Department truck, onto the small dirt front yard. The fire is now blazing through the two upstairs dormer windows.

The rescue squad can only look on in horror -- all except one -- ambulance driver, Gary Sikes, who helps fireman Gary Watts, get a ladder up to the front upstairs window where the mother says her children are trapped.

Tabor City police officers Russell and Moyer, who have twice tried to go upstairs to rescue the children tell the firemen they had also attempted to enter the house by the side door to the kitchen, but a table was up against the locked door.

As the firemen go up ladders, ambulance crew Melissa Sikes and Lorrie Lancaster, standing beside their ambulance, try to get information from the mother, who won't get off her cordless phone long enough to answer their questions.

The mother is walking around the ambulance while she talks on the phone. Melissa Sikes overhears the mother say, "My babies are burned." (At this point, the Fowlers are still inside looking for the children).

Finally, the mother acknowledges that there are two

children in the house. Lorrie Lancaster loans the mother her black jacket to wear.

Immediately, Lorrie Lancaster calls the 911 dispatcher to ask for an additional ambulance.

Lorrie then asks the mother to get in the front seat of the ambulance so that as soon as the children were brought out, they can rush to the hospital.

The mother refuses: "I'm going to wait for my boyfriend." She then walks down the road toward the neighbor's driveway, across the street.

At 4:06, Tracey Fowler rushes out of the house carrying a lifeless, little, blond-haired, girl. Tracey hands the little girl to ambulance driver Gary Sikes, who feels how limp she is. She's wearing blue, one-piece, footed pajamas. There are no signs of burning, but she reeks of smoke.

Sikes lays the child on the stretcher inside the ambulance, calls out to the mother, who is by now, 20 yards down the road heading toward the Lewis's yard across the street. "Let's go. Hurry!"

She yells back, "I'm waiting for my boyfriend."

Inside the ambulance, Lorrie Lancaster is able to get a pulse on four-year-old Brittany Hinson -- a very low pulse.

She places an oropharyngeal in Brittany's mouth. Melissa Sikes starts using the bag valve mask 100%, while Lorrie Lancaster monitors Brittany's pulse and holds her neck in a neutral position. Both women are crying, sobbing, and pleading, "Please breathe, little girl. Please breathe!"

Brittany lies motionless, reeking of smoke, too small and innocent to be so close to death.

The nearest hospital is across the state line in Loris, South Carolina. All the way there, Melissa Sikes and Lorrie Lancaster talk through their tears to the little girl, praying she will live.

The ambulance arrives at the Loris Community Hospital emergency dock at 4:13. Brittany is alive! Her pulse is steady! She's breathing –fighting for her life against carbon monoxide drowning her lungs. She's placed on a ventilator.

Medical Transport of Horry County, South Carolina, will airlift Brittany to Charleston Medical Hospital Children's Burn Center. (Brittany's mother does not accompany her drowning daughter to either Loris Community Hospital or Charleston's Children's Burn Center.)

Gary Watts -- firemen/ambulance driver -- picks up the barely recognizable, badly burned baby, rushed it to the second ambulance, jumped in, and roared off for Loris Community Hospital, while Ronnie and Sondra Watts start CPR on little Josh Hinson, only 17 months old, who is in full cardiac arrest with burns so severe, his little body, barely recognizable, is blackened from head to toe.

Lt. Michael Glenn is awakened by the 911 call. When he arrives at 101 South Wall St., the house is in flames. The fire trucks and one ambulance are on the scene.

Corporal Annie Gause is interviewing a white adult female in the front yard. The woman is upset, but not crying. She has a cordless phone in her hand. Corporal Gause identifies her as the mother of the two children who are trapped inside the burning house, Brittany, age 4, and Josh, age 17 months.

Corporal Gause advises Lt. Glenn that Brittany is en route to Loris Community Hospital.

Firefighter Gary Watts is placing the second child in the ambulance. (In his report, Lt. Glenn states the child's clothes have "melted and adhered to the skin.")

A male neighbor approaches from the house across the street and invites the mother, Terri Hinson, to go to his home to calm down.

Lt. Glenn accompanies Terri Hinson to the Lewis home. She tells Glenn, "I sleep downstairs 2 - 3 times a week." She explains that the house was cold, so she used a space heater in the upstairs hallway. (When Patrolman

Russell and Moyer tried to go up the stairs to rescue the children, they both reported seeing orange flames UNDER the door of the bedroom straight ahead -- Josh's bedroom -- meaning the door was shut, causing the police to wonder why Josh's door would be shut, when the only source of heat was from a space heater in the hall.)

Terri Hinson tells Lt. Glenn that she heard her daughter crying and went to check on her. When she reached the top of the stairs, she saw a flash and flames coming from the closet area of her son's bedroom. She ran down the stairs and called 911.

Lt. Glenn notes that Ms. Hinson's hair is singed and her face is red and "pasty".

"Someone told me the fire was electrical," she informs Lt. Glenn, "caused by the heater upstairs." (At that point, Hinson has not discussed the cause of the fire with anyone.) She adds that she may have moved the downstairs heater when the policemen first tried to go up the stairs and that the heater was cold because the power went off. (Police and firemen recall the lights were on downstairs when they arrived and right up until the time they pulled the electric box. Furthermore, if she didn't move the heater out of the way until the policemen needed it moved to get upstairs, does that mean the mother never tried to go up the stairs herself?)

Hinson ends the interview when her boyfriend comes to pick her up. There was an older woman in the car, presumably Terri Hinson's mother.

Lt. Glenn then calls patrolman Ramey, who had rented the house before Hinson. Ramey says the circuit breakers kept switching off, a lot of the outlets didn't work, and most of the switches were loose and needed replacement. Ramey recalls he had never seen any sparks or experienced wires getting hot. Later, officer Ramey would tell investigators that he had installed about four smoke detectors in the house. (At the time of the fire, none were found.)

11

Both Police Chief Wooster and Fire Chief Watts, tell Glenn, the fire started in the right corner of Josh's bedroom closet in, or around, a pile of clothes.

Lt. Glenn has yellow crime scene tape placed around the front lawn area, including a silver Cougar parked in the Hinson driveway. The fire scene is left unattended.

4:21 A.M., seven minutes later, Gary Watts pulls into the Loris Community Hospital emergency docking area. Josh is still in cardiac arrest. They lay Josh in the room next to his sister, Brittany, who is fighting for her life.

At 4:23, Josh is placed on a monitor -- asystolic. At 4:28 intubation is attempted -- unsuccessful. 4:34: A second intubation is unsuccessful, IV cannot be started. CPR continues --oxygen at 15L/min.

4:38 Joshua Cade Hinson, age 17 months, is pronounced DOA. Cause of death: Carbon monoxide poisoning.

Thirty-five minutes after Brittany arrived and 27 minutes after Josh arrived or, 4:48 Sunday morning, Brittany and Josh's mother shows up at the Emergency Room accompanied by her mother, Bernice Hinson Prince, and boyfriend Rodney Strickland. (Hinson would later claim it took the rescue squad 48 minutes to arrive at the fire. She had the time right, but the circumstance wrong, it had taken Hinson 48 minutes to get to the hospital where one of her children was fighting for its life and her other child had lost his fight.)

Lorrie Lancaster, who had given the mother her black jacket to wear back at the house, goes into the Triage Room to retrieve her coat and replace it with a blanket, at which time, the mother offers, "I was asleep on the couch when the fire started."

The ambulance crew, who had worked so hard to save baby Josh, now has to drive him to the Columbus County Morgue, where his little lifeless body will lie, before transporting him to the Chief Medical Examiner at the University of North Carolina Medical School in Chapel Hill.

On their way back to Tabor City, Melissa Sikes, Lorrie Lancaster, and Gary Sikes share their observation that Josh's mother was faking -- working too hard to convince people she's a grieving mother -- that she's really a whole lot less upset than other folks they've dealt with in far less tragic circumstances.

The Autopsy

Seven hours after Josh was pronounced DOA, the Medical Examiner writes, "The decedent is clothed only in the charred remains of a blue sleep suit. The body is that of a white male infant, which is extremely sooted. There is focal skin slippage. There is light charring of the fingers. Apart from thermal damage, there is no evidence of injury ... Examination shows deposition of soot in the airways. There are no premortem injuries ... Carbon monoxide is detected at a saturation of greater than 70%. Death is due to carbon monoxide poisoning sustained in a house fire. The presence of an elevated carbon monoxide shows the decedent was alive at the beginning of the fire and died as a result of the fire. The thermal damage is, therefore, postmortem. At this time arson is suspected."

The State's Investigation

Later, that same morning, around 7:35 A.M., (Sunday) Corporal Gause, off-duty and driving by the burned house, calls into Officer Russell that, "Subjects had crossed the yellow tape and were in the residence."

When Officer Russell arrives, he sees a man and a woman loading items from the residence into a silver Cougar. He recognizes the woman as Terri Hinson. Russell stops. He advises the two that the tape is a warning to keep anyone from trespassing, entering the house, or removing anything from it. He tells them to go to the police department.

At the police station, Hinson explains she'd gone to the house to pick up some clothes, get the car, and get video tapes to take to Brittany at the Burn Center. (In fact, she didn't go to the Burn Center that morning.)

She tells Lt. Glenn, "I intentionally sleep downstairs because the electrical plug on the heater might spark and

cause a problem. The wire felt hot before the fire started."
She then wonders aloud how the fire could have started in the
closet as there are no outlets, switches, or even lights in there.

She also could not explain how Josh's bedroom door
could have been closed as police officers Moyer and Russell
reported, when she always left it open because it was
extremely hard to open or close because of the rug. (She had
told Officer Gause she had closed both bedroom doors
because "it was so hot in the children's rooms.")

The man, identified as Rodney Strickland, tells Tabor
City Police Chief Wooster that he pays the rent for the 101
South Wall Street house to a Mike Jones, owner of Jones
Department Stores. Strickland acknowledges he lives with
Terri Hinson, pays her bills, including her car payment, but
that everything is in her name. (Both Hinson and Strickland
would later report that Rodney has a Workman's Comp claim
pending, noting, he's too injured to work.) Strickland says
further that Terri Hinson, receives child support, welfare,
student aid, and gets some help from her mother.

Finally, Strickland tells Chief Wooster that he was
exercising his weekend overnight visitation rights with his
teenage son, 15 miles up the road in Fair Bluff, the night of
the fire.

At 11:15 a.m., the morning of the fire, Special Agent
T. K. West, of the North Carolina Bureau of Investigation,
interviews North Carolina Highway patrolman Jon Lewis,
who resides at 201 East Fifth Street, Tabor City, NC. The side
of his house faces South Wall Street and the front of the
Hinson house across the road.

Lewis tells Special Agent West he was awakened
around 4:00, early Sunday morning, October 20, by the sound
of an emergency vehicle siren, a large vehicle stopping, and a
woman screaming. From his bedroom window, he saw rescue
vehicles parked on Wall Street and fire coming from the back
of Terri Hinson's house.

Once outside, Lewis sees Terri standing in front of her house talking to a Tabor City police officer. As he approaches, both Terri and the policeman tell him that the children are still inside. Lewis offers assistance and his home to Terri.

Lewis notes that Terri seems hysterical, but not crying. She keeps saying, "I don't know why I didn't get my babies out."

Later, accompanied by Tabor City policeman Lt. Glenn, Lewis, his wife Jamie, and Terri goes inside the Lewis's home, where Lt. Glenn interviews Terri with Mrs. Lewis present.

The Lewis' tell Agent West that neither he nor his wife had any real contact with Terri, her children, or the man living with Terri, other than to say hello in passing. Lewis had heard that the man living with Terri was married to a woman up the road in Fair Bluff, with their two sons. Terri, her children, and the man, had moved in about four or five months ago. During that time, a private investigator had asked Lewis if he'd seen the man doing any strenuous work because the man had filed a Workman's Compensation claim stating he was unable to work. Lewis told the detective he'd seen the man mowing the yard and doing other strenuous yard work.

Lewis recalls that before he went to work at 8 AM on the morning after the fire, he saw the man removing clothing and other items from Terri's house and putting them in a silver Cougar that both he and Terri drive.

Jamie Lewis recounts that Terri keeps a dog chained in the yard all day. On several occasions, Mrs. Lewis had asked Terri to unchain the dog and play with it because no one ever did. That was the only real contact the Lewis's had with Terri or her boyfriend.

Mrs. Lewis adds that she sat with Terri Hinson while Hinson was being interviewed by a Tabor City policeman.

She heard Terri say that she fell asleep downstairs because there was something electrical downstairs that she did not trust. During the night, she said she heard her little girl calling her, and when the mother heard a "woosh" sound, she knew there was a fire. She had used a space heater upstairs, "but she went upstairs and saw the heater and it was ok."

Hinson said that her son was "such a pretty little boy that she could not believe that she had lost him."

Terri was not crying or hysterical, but upset.

Terri's "hair was singed all over her head, but she did not appear to have any injuries." Terri carried a cordless telephone in her hand and a cigarette case, and Terri wore prescription glasses, but was not wearing them during the time Terri was in the Lewis home.

About five minutes after the police officer left, or around 4:30, Terri Hinson walked outside where Terri was met by a woman Jamie assumed was Terri's mother and a man she thought was her father. When the woman asked Terri about the children, Terri replied, "No one will tell me anything."

A female police officer approached and asked if she could help. Terri asked to see her children. The police officer told Terri the children had been transported to the hospital in Loris, South Carolina. Terri then asked if she could go to the hospital, to which the female officer said, "Of course." Terri then left with the man and woman.

Around noon, the morning of the fire, SBI Agent T.K. West interviewed Tabor City Police Lt. Michael Glenn, who reports that patrol office Annie Gause was already conducting preliminary interviews when he arrived at the fire scene. At that time, the children had not been found. When Glenn first spoke to Terri Hinson, he observed she was not tearful, but she was "upset." She was carrying a cordless phone in her hand. He encouraged her to go with her neighbor over to his house to "calm down." Glenn went to the Lewis home where he interviewed Terri Hinson, who told Lt. Glenn the house was cold and that she had used a space heater upstairs in the hallway and downstairs in the living room, and that she had moved the downstairs heater out of the way so they (the policemen) could get up the stairs to rescue the children, and when she moved it, the heater was cold, meaning the " power must have gone off." (No, the light in the living room where the heater was located was still on.)

Glenn went on to tell SBI Agent West that the crime scene was left unattended after the firefighters left and that the yellow tape had been around the front yard of the Hinson residence including a silver Cougar parked in the driveway. Around 8:00 a.m. that same morning, Officer Russell checked the residence where Terri Hinson and Rodney Strickland were observed "carrying items from the residence and putting them in the Cougar. Russell stopped them and told them to meet him at the police station, where Hinson told Glenn they were picking up some clothes, videotapes for Brittany they were going to take to Brittany at the burn center in Charleston, as soon as they got their things, and the Cougar. (Terri never went to the Burn Center that morning or even that afternoon.)

Lt. Glenn concluded his interview by advising Agent West that he had contacted DSS regarding what had happened to the other three Hinson children, but was told to call back Monday.

On October 21, Lt. Glenn interviewed Rodney Strickland., who said he left that Saturday morning around 11:30 to drive to Fair Bluff for visitation with his 14-year old son, Jeremy, at the home of his ex-wife. He spent that night at his mother's house in Fair Bluff. Early the next morning, Terri called to tell him the house was on fire and the children were trapped inside.

Strickland told Glenn, "I'm under constant pressure" and couldn't explain what caused the fire. Strickland also said there were no smoke detectors, but that he had been "meaning to install some." He went on to say that "Terri went upstairs and saw a flash from the closet."

Rodney Strickland next claimed the doctor told them, "There was no hurry to get to Charleston as there was little they could do." Rodney and Terri drove to her mother's in Fair Bluff "to stay with family and rest until 3:00 PM, at which time, they were to drive to Charleston. (Strickland claimed to have asked the police permission to enter the house to get belongings. The police have no record of such a request, and would not have granted it, as arson and murder were suspected.)

"I don't know of any reason for the fire to have started and me and Terri had been thinking about how it did,"

Strickland concluded the interview by saying, "Terri had gotten pregnant by this man named Kenneth Bryant, who took off to Georgia and denied the child was his. Terri was alone. We became friends." (Coleman would learn almost two years later that Terri Hinson had volunteered to both Kenneth Bryant and his mother that Terri had undergone kidney surgery which left her "unable to have any more kids," thus misleading Mr. Bryant to conclude any sex with Terri would be "safe sex.")

On October 22, around 10:15 A.M., North Carolina State Bureau of Investigation Agent Matt White interviewed Terri Louise Hinson, W/F/DOB: 4/24/64, in White's vehicle.

Hinson reported, that on the Saturday afternoon before the fire, she had just returned home after taking her boyfriend, Rodney Strickland, to his mother's house in Fair Bluff, (where he would be spending the night in order to exercise his weekend visitation rights with his teenage son). Joshua Hinson had made the trip, too.

Josh and his mother returned at approximately 12:30, Saturday afternoon.

Brittany Hinson, the four-year-old daughter was with

her grandmother, Bernice Hinson Prince, who returned Brittany home about 5:30 that same Saturday afternoon.

Mother and grandmother fed the children, then Terri "did" her mother's hair, after which, the grandmother went home to her residence in Flair Bluff.

Terri Hinson continued her account of the events by stating she had an electrical heater plugged into the downstairs electrical outlet near the front door. She claims the heater cord running between the electric heater and the extension cord, which was plugged into the wall behind the couch, was hot when she touched it. She felt the cord because it was in the way of the front door when her mother left to go home. She also touched the outlet behind the couch. It was hot, too. (NEMAX fire investigators would find the heaters had been turned to their maximum setting, yet the mother would report at one time she'd closed the children's bedroom doors because their room had gotten so hot, only to contradict herself again by telling law enforcement she always left the children's bedroom doors open and didn't know how Josh's door had been closed.)

Hinson next told SBI Agent White that she stayed downstairs after putting the children to bed because she was scared the heater downstairs might catch on fire. (Why then use it at all and instead go upstairs to bed where it would be safe?)

She'd put the children to bed around 7:00 PM. (Friends would later report that Terri typically put her children to bed between 6-7, "to get them out of her way.")

She now tells Special Agent White that she'd also placed a heater on the upstairs landing area, at an angle to heat both of the children's bedrooms, (Why then was Josh's door closed?) and plugged it into an outlet on the wall near the top of the stairs.

She'd stayed downstairs to work on a research paper for her class at Southeastern Community College where she was a criminal justice major.

Sometime between 10:30 and 11:00, she reports hearing her son Josh "call out." She picked up a small flashlight from the top of the entertainment center and walked upstairs to check on him. (When asked why she didn't simply turn on the light on the stairs, she said there was no light for the stairs. However, Coleman's later photo shows the light switch on the wall at the bottom of the stairs.)

The mother goes on to say that she found Josh lying on his left side with a pacifier in his mouth and a bottle in his right arm. A stuffed rabbit was in his left arm. He was "fast asleep."

She then flashed the light around the room to check for spiders. She doesn't see any. She also checked a spot in his room where some water damage had occurred and caused a bow in the ceiling in his room, before returning downstairs.

Around 12:30 A.M., Sunday morning, she claims she laid down on the couch and fell asleep.

The next thing she remembers is being awoken by Brittany calling, "Mamma, I'm scared!"

When she opened her eyes, she saw a reddish/orange glow coming from upstairs. (Impossible to see up the stairs from her place around the corner on the sofa.) She heard the crackling of the fire. She ran upstairs and ducked down at the landing. Josh's door is open. (Police and firefighters found his door closed.) When she got to the doorjamb area, "The fire goes whoosh". She felt the heat coming out of the room. The fire came out above her head, singing her hair. (SBI Agent Matt White does not see any burns or singed hair.) Hinson explains she had a friend fix her hair before the interview.

She claims that she tried to get to her daughter, but the girl's room was too full of smoke.

Twice, she heard Josh call, "Mamma." She said she couldn't get in the room because the fire was coming out of

21

Josh's closet and spreading. (How did she know that without being able to see into the room? Did she then close the door?)

Brittany kept saying, "I'm scared." Her mother tells the SBI that she called to her daughter to come to her, but she wouldn't. She then went downstairs, grabbed the cordless phone, called 911, then went back upstairs with the phone. (On the tape of the 911 call, Hinson says she's downstairs and can't get upstairs to get the children.)

She tells SBI Agent White, the 911 dispatcher told her to get out of the house. (Not according to the tape. Besides, she was in the house when the police arrived.)

She had noticed a police car next door, (from the front window looking out?), the downstairs heater was in the way of the front door, so she grabbed it to let the policeman enter and thinks it strange that the heater is cold, reasoning the power must have gone off. (If so, why was the upstairs heater still running and the light on downstairs?)

One police officer tried to go upstairs but is turned back by the smoke. Fire trucks arrived. Firemen go to the windows to try to rescue the children.

Next, she tells SBI Agent White that the house is rented from Mike Jones, owner of Jones Department Stores and attorney Richard Wright, for $240 per month. Her boyfriend, Rodney Strickland pays the rent -- $60 per week. She says there have been no problems with the electricity, although sometimes after Hurricane Fran, the lights in the living room would flicker.

Hinson claims that Rodney Strickland was going to adopt her children, and that three other children of hers, Bradley, Timmy, and Ashley Tripp had all been adopted, but that she had been "forced" to give up her children or lose them to Social Services. She admits she signed the adoption papers, but claims she had gone to Charlotte to find work and was going to send for her children. (Mr. Tripp and her mother contend she'd run off to Charlotte with a new boyfriend and essentially abandoned Bradley, Timmy, and Ashley.)

Terri Hinson then tells Agent White she considered suicide when she found out she was pregnant with Brittany.

At the time of the fire, Terri Hinson acknowledged getting a Welfare check of $236 a month, plus a PELL Grant for her courses at Southeastern Community College, and that her boyfriend pays her rent and bills from the Workman's Comp he has been receiving for two years, with a "lump sum settlement due any time now."

On October 22, SBI Agent Mathews and USF&G adjuster Steve Magini interviewed Terri Hinson who tells them, "I had a little flashlight I picked up 'cause I didn't want to turn any lights on and wake the kids up and ah ... I went up there (Josh's room) and looked at him and he was fine and he was on his side. He was asleep ... I covered him up ... I didn't use the baseboard heat because I know it's dangerous ...It wouldn't heat the upstairs ...I laid on the couch on my right side. I heard Brittany call out, 'Mommy, I'm scared!' I opened my eyes and I could see to the top of the stairs" (impossible from the couch over on the right side of the room) "and I could see a red-orange glow and I knew what was going on just by seeing the color ... I ran ... I saw the glow and I ran ... and, ahem... I saw the flames coming out. It looked like it was coming from his closet area ... you know ... shooting out towards him ... so I ... at that point, I knew the flames weren't in Brittany's room. It was in his room. I couldn't stand up in his room and a lot of smoke and ah... I got to his door. I got right at his door. It was open. It was not all the way open ... You couldn't -- His door would open where it would touch the other wall. But, the carpet ... I think it was new when we moved in, or fairly new, and it was hard to open that door past a certain point so I never opened it all the way back ..."

Next, Special Agent Matt Mathews and adjuster Steve

Magini interview Terri Hinson's live-in boyfriend Rodney Strickland, who tells the Matthews and Magini, "I was asleep on the couch at my mother's. Something, for some reason or another it was – might have been minutes before ... I wake up and get some water and laid back down and the phone rang – my mother has gotten prank calls 2:00, 3:00, 4:00 in the morning – Terri says, "Come home! Come home! The house is on fire and I can't get my babies.!""

I went to my mother's room and asked for her cars keys. The phone rang again. It was Terri's mother saying she was coming by and would pick me up. She doesn't drive too well at night, so I told her to stop and let me drive. "I was fully dressed. I didn't intend to go to sleep on the sofa because I got a bedroom there. The call came in a few minutes before 4:00 AM. Probably by the time we got there it may have been a quarter after 4:00. The patrolman's wife was with Terri. The ambulances had already left. I'd gone out for cigars around 9:30 Saturday night.

Later that same day, SBI Agent Matt White, accompanied by USF&G adjuster, Steve Magini, interviewed Terri Hinson at her mother's home in Fair Bluff, NC.

Q.   Terri, I am speaking with you today concerning a fire that occurred and my understanding is that you were staying at the home at 101 Wall Street in Tabor City?

A.   Yes, sir.

Q.   Okay. Do you know approximately what time?

A.   I remember somebody in the hospital saying they got the call to 911 at 3:47

Q.   Okay. 3:47?

A.   It's the time they said I called them and they said they were there at 3:49.

Q.   Okay. I would like for you to describe for me the sequence of events going on say ... Saturday from lunch until ... We will get up to the fire, but what was going on Saturday? Where were you Saturday? Where were you staying?... that type of thing?

A. Ahm ... I was down there that morning ... ah ... we have another car there at the home and it's not tagged yet, and we were going to do that this week ... and ah, we only had one car, and I brought Rodney with the Cougar back to his mom's because he had to visit his son that night and ah ... I brought my daughter here because she wanted to spend some time with her "Meema." That's the normal thing every Saturday. Mom would keep her for a few hours. So, I brought her back here and I think I got home ... back there somewhere around 12:30 ...somewhere in that area.

Q. Okay. How many children do you have?

A. I have two living with ... well ... Brittany and Josh were living with me. I have three others that were adopted.

Q. Okay. Where was Joshua at the time you brought Brittany by here?

A. With me. Joshua went with me everywhere ... (laughs) ... It didn't matter where I went, he was with me. I mean, that's just always been.

Q. So what time did you get back to the house Saturday evening?

A. I think I got back about 12:30 and he already had lunch so I laid him down for a nap and he went on to sleep and everything was fine. And I fixed me something to eat for lunch and then started working on some homework I had for school.

Q. Where are you in school?

A. Southeastern Community College.

Q. Okay. What are you taking there?

A. Criminal justice. Up until this quarter and then I switched to teaching. I want to go and get ... wanted to go and get a psychology Masters and do forensic psychology or something. So kinda connect the law somewhere down the line.

Q. Okay. Rodney mentioned that he was also in

community college, What is he in?

A. He's in criminal justice. (Laughs) He's going to graduate before I do and he started way after I did.

Q. Okay. You went back to the house about 12-12:30 Saturday. What happened the remainder of the afternoon?

A. Basically, when he got up from his nap, we just played a little while like we always did ...

Q. What time did he get up?

A. Probably around three. He usually took about a two-hour nap. Ah ... I wouldn't let him sleep too long in the afternoons. But, ah ... I heard him upstairs. He was talking to the dog again. He always got up and looked out and talked to the dog.

Q. And you two were the only ones home at the time?

A. Yeah ... and we didn't leave the house anymore, at all. My mother brought Brittany home ... ah ... I know that sounds strange, I call everything home. But she brought her down here. I think it was around 5 ... between 5 and 6 somewhere in that area ... I vaguely remember that.

Q. Was Rodney home at the time?

A. He was at his mom's.

Q. When did he leave?

A. That morning ... I brought him over there ... he had to be there by 12:00 ... I think we got there -- I don't know -- sometime before 12:00.

Q. Okay. So, basically ah ... it wound up with you, Joshua and Brittany back at the house about what time?

A. Well, all three of us and Mom ... We were all there ... She got there like I said between five and six -- sometime in that area. And, then I gave them all supper and Mom ate some supper with me and then she helped me get them ready for bed. And, I put Brittany down ... and I believe that ... I'm kinda vague on it but I think that – ahm... I had did Mom's hair and all that stuff before I laid them down. I mean, I usually fix my Mom's hair about once a week. When I did that I had felt the heater ... I don't know if ya'll have been in at all ... if they let ya'll in or ...

Q. We did get in, yes.

A. I had a heater ... It's like an oil stand up heater there and it's plugged into an outlet behind the love seat.

Q. This is the den you're talking about?

A. Yeah, and I plugged a curling iron into the same outlet and I noticed it was kinda warm feeling when I plugged it in ... so I felt of the cord.

Q. What is it? It was ...

A. Down ... You know -- as I got to it, it felt a little warm ... I mean, this was in the evening -- early evening. And, ah ... I felt the cord to the heater and it felt warm ... and ah ... I remember mentioning to mom; I said, I need to talk to Rodney.

Q. Was the heater on?

A. Yeah, it was on ... It was pretty cool. I'm a very cold natured person and I believe in everybody staying warm, so –

Q. Could the heater have possibly been heating up the wall?

A. No, I don't think so.

Q. And the outlet? Which outlet was the heater plugged into?

A. There are not that many outlets in that house, but it was the one behind the love seat.

Q. The one under the window?

A. Yeah. And ah ... but I remember then, yeah, I told Mom then about saying something to Rodney about it because it wasn't normal for that cord to be hot. I mean I never had that kind of trouble with anything. And, ah ... because of that I went ahead and put them to bed and Mom came on home and ah ...

Q. What time did you put Brittany to bed?

A. They both went down around 7:00. Somewhere in that area.

Q.   You put them down together?

A.   Yeah, at the same time. They ah ... Joshua would go to bed anytime you said it. If you said the word "Night-night", ... he would go to bed. The kid loved to go to bed. But, ah ... I was determined that he was going to stay up past seven. I could never get Brittany to stay up past seven. She was just ... they just didn't want to go ... stay up ... (laughs).

Q.   So, they went to bed early like that normally?

A.   Oh yeah. ...But, then they got up early, too, because I had to get up early and go to school.

Q.   Joshua sleep through the night now?

A.   Oh yeah. Gosh, he started sleeping through the night when he was real young ... younger than normal ... But, they thought that was because he was low birth weight and he slept anyway because that's all he could do and they think it just kept on with him.

Q.   Okay. So you put both of them to bed around 7:00.

A.   Right.

Q.   What did you do at that time? What did you do, from say 7:00 until 9:00?

A.   I went back downstairs and every two weeks we have to do a report for one of my classes and my mom saves the newspapers because it had to be something in the news, so I was going through two weeks of newspapers because I had to get my report ready for that class and ah... my brother called and I talked to him for a little while and ah... after I talked to him, I went back to the newspapers for a few minutes and then I decided I needed to iron some clothes, you know, to wear for next week, or this week...

Q.   Okay. Where did you sit the ironing board and where did you plug it in?

A.   It was plugged in next to the entertainment center.

Q.   Okay. And, where did you sit the ironing board?

A.   The ironing board was in front like at an angle... the ah... and I was sitting here trying to think when I went back in the house over there I don't remember seeing my iron, but after I finished ironing I'd always sit my iron up on the stairs right here so I could get to it ...

Q. I saw an iron somewhere today.

A. Well, I had two. I had one upstairs that I never used.

Q. I believe the one upstairs is the one I saw.

A. I never use that iron. I don't know how I ended up with two irons to start with (laughs).

Q. About what time did you finish ironing?

A. I was watching TV at the same time and I think I turned the TV off somewhere around 10-10:30 or 11 -- somewhere in that area.

Q. What time did your Mom leave?

A. Ah ... I have no idea ... It wasn't long after the kids went to bed. She just ... She didn't like being out too much after dark. She doesn't drive too well in the dark.

Q. Okay. After you finished ironing and turned the TV off, was it just you and the two kids at home?

A. Yeah ... ah ... I heard Joshua cry out, which I found very strange.

Q About what time?

A. I think it was about 10:30 or 11 -- somewhere in that area -- around the same time I was putting everything up.

Q. Okay. Did you go upstairs at that time?

A. I had a little handheld flashlight I picked up because I didn't want to turn any lights on and wake the kids up and ah... I picked it up and went up there and looked at him and he was fine and he was laying on his side asleep. I don't know. He just called out for some reason and I just made sure he was Okay. I covered him up I made sure he had his blanket on him, his rabbit, his bottle and his... ah... I am real paranoid about spiders, and that house had a lot of spiders in it periodically. It's like when Fran came through they were coming from everywhere. They were coming through the wood and I don't know... what ya'll can tell now -- I don't remember... a while ago... but in the upstairs room there are crevices all around the wall and they would come out of there so I spray around there real good making sure they were out and when I checked on them, I remember taking the flashlight and looking around to make sure there weren't no spiders and I didn't see any.

Q. This was about 10:30...?

A. Yeah... and I went back to ah... for some reason, I couldn't sleep. I was real restless.

Q. Okay.

A. And ah... stayed up probably to around 12 or 12:30, I think...

Q. What were you doing say between 10:30 after you checked on Joshua and 12:00?

A. I went back to going through the newspapers that I had put down earlier and I had a real hard time trying to find something to write a paper on.

Q. Okay. Sitting up reading those?

A. Yeah and uh... I just got tired. So, I laid down on the couch and I didn't want to sleep upstairs because of the ah... heater. I felt like, I don't know, I just had a feeling that something might happen with that heater with that cord being hot and I felt like if I was there with it and something happened, I could do something about it.

Q. Do you not have a heating system upstairs?

A. It had ah... I think it's called baseboard heat, but I didn't feel good about that. I've never... that kind of heat I know is dangerous and I didn't feel good about using that kind of heat.

Q. How about the heater upstairs? Is it just like the one downstairs? Does that not give enough heat? In other words, why did you leave the heater on downstairs?

A. Because it doesn't heat... it would heat like that area there -- the living room and kitchen, but it wouldn't go upstairs enough and I wanted to make sure they were warm,

30

so I kept one up there, you know, to keep those rooms and ah
...

Q.   But you felt like you needed to keep both of them
on?

A.   Yeah... I just... I knew they were calling for some
real cold weather that night; it was supposed to get real cold
and I didn't want them...

Q.   Were both of them on when you finally laid down at
12 or 12:30?

A.   Yeah, they were on. I don't think I had the one
upstairs turned up too high... but I think... I really don't
remember. Ahm... but I felt like something about that heater,
because of the cord... I just didn't feel good.

Q.   When you normally stay there, is it customary for
you to sleep downstairs on the couch?

A.   No... If anything... when he would study, I would
fall asleep on the couch and then he would wake me up when
he got ready for bed. We would go to bed.

Q.   Okay. Upstairs?

A.   Yeah, because he...

Q.   Is it customary for ya'll to leave when you and he ...
when he would be studying and you would fall asleep on the
couch and he would wake you up to go upstairs, and
everybody ended up upstairs? Was it customary to leave that
heater on downstairs?

A.   Not usually.

Q.   Okay. On this particular night... why did you not
turn off the downstairs... and I'm not questioning you, I'm
just asking... Why did you not turn off the downstairs heater
and simply use the upstairs heating system? Why did you
decide to leave the downstairs?

A.   I don't know how to answer that?

Q.   Okay.

A.   I really don't know.

Q.   That's understandable.

A. I just don't have an answer.

Q. Okay. Ah... you went to bed around 12 or 12:30?

A. Yeah... I laid down on the couch somewhere around there and I was laying on my right side.

Q. Okay. When you went to bed what lights went out? What lights were left on I should say?

A. Ah... I think the lamp on my entertainment center was on. I usually ...

Q. How about upstairs?

A. No, there were no lights on upstairs.

Q. Okay. Any baseboard heat being used upstairs?

A. No. To my knowledge, those heaters have never been turned on at all since we've been there.

Q. Okay. Any ah... lamps or anything left on upstairs?

A. No.

Q. Any fans?

A. No. The only thing on was that heater. That only heater in the hall. And, I had an alarm clock in the bedroom.

Q. Okay. You decided to sleep on the sofa downstairs and describe ...

A. Big mistake...

Q. ...The next thing that you recall?

A. I heard Brittany call out "Mommy, I'm scared" and I opened my eyes and the angle that I was laying, I was able to see almost at the top of the stairs and I could just see a red-orange glow and I knew what was going on just by seeing the color.

Q. Sure, sure, go ahead... so you heard Brittany call your name?

A. Yeah... she... ah... called my name and I looked up and I knew when I saw the color what was happening.

Q. Okay. Does Brittany normally go up and down the stairs by herself?

A. Yeah. She normally does.

Q. Okay. If she ever wakes up and... okay...

A.   Well, first, Brittany never got up in the middle of the night.

Q.   Okay.

A.   She would sleep until probably 6:00 or 6:30 depending on what time I had to be at school the next morning. I might have to go in and wake her up.

Q.   Okay, so you heard her call your name. What did you do at that time?

A.   I ran... I saw the glow and I ran... and ahm...

Q.   Where did you run?

A.   When I started heading up the stairs, I saw the flames coming out it looked like from his closet area... you know... shooting out towards him... so I... at that point, I knew the flames weren't in Brittany's room -- it was in his room.

Q.   You knew the flames were not in Brittany's room?

A.   Yeah, so I headed for his room and I ran... and I couldn't stand up -- it was too hot... I   couldn't stand up in his room and a lot of smoke... a lot of smoke and ah...

Q.   Did you get to the top of the stairs?

A.   Oh yeah. I got to his door. I got right at his door.

Q.   (Magini) Was his door open or closed?

A.   It was open. It was... not all the way open... you couldn't. His door would open where it would touch the other wall. But the carpet... I think it was new when we moved in or fairly new and it was hard to open that door past a certain, so I never opened it all the way back so it was opened like this. If you walked in, it was like a straight angle from the door, I mean you could walk in and it was straight over.

Q.   Alright.

A.   And ah... no, I didn't get into his room. I was kinda scooting down trying to get in and as soon as I got right at his door, it was like a loud ... the only way I could explain it was like a loud   "wooshing" sound and it went right over me. It came out into the hall ... the fire started coming out into the

33

hall. And I had to turn back and I tried to get into Brittany's room and I couldn't find her. I couldn't see her and all I could do is holler for her and I told her to come to me and she wouldn't come to me and I couldn't find her. I couldn't see anything. And, so I ran downstairs into the kitchen and I picked up the cordless phone and I was talking to them when I went up the second time and I couldn't get any further and I couldn't get past the top step. I mean, that was as far as I could go. And the cops come in and they made me leave and go out and ah... I remember one of them going up ... trying to go up and then coming out saying, "I can't get in. The odd thing I remembered we were coming back to Charleston or coming back from Charleston later that day... ahm... that I hadn't thought of earlier – is that the heater downstairs, when I was going out the door when they told me to leave out of the house, I remember it was so ... it was right there and it could be in somebody's way and I remember picking it up and moving it, so it wouldn't get in anybody's way.

Q.   Uh-huh...

A.   That heater would take a good hour to hour and a half to two hours to cool off to where I could have done that. And it was cold, so ...

Q.   Was the lamp still on?

A.   There was nothing on ... it was dark. The only light I think ... I believe the woman across in the upstairs apartment had a light on outside and I think some light was coming from that.

Q.   When you got to the top of the stairs the first time, was Brittany still crying?

A.   She called, "Mommy, I'm scared!" I heard her twice. And, I heard him twice."

Q.   Okay.

A.   I heard him call "Momma" twice. (Voice breaks)

Q.   You heard Joshua as well?

A.   (Answer unintelligible)

34

Q. Okay. When you checked on Joshua at 10:30, did you go back upstairs for any reason or anytime other than the time you went up the first time that the fire was going on? In other words, between 10:30, between 10:30 and the time the fire occurred, did you go ...?

A. I want to say I went back up and checked on him before I laid down around midnight or 12:30 -- somewhere in that area. Seems like I went back up one more time ...

Q. Try to narrow it down.

A. ...because he had laid down, I mean, because he had cried out before I had felt like. I think I went back up one more time. I'm not going to swear to it, but I honestly think I did. I would have done that normally.

Q. Okay. Try to recall if you did go back up to check on him at 10:30, was he cold at that time? In other words, did you put another blanket on him at that time?

A. No ... he had a ah ... I wouldn't even ... I don't know if you even want to call it a blanket. I did... it was a... ah ... top of a flannel sheet. The top part, not the fitted part. That is actually what I covered him up in and it had gone down to the end of the crib.

Q. Okay.

A. So, I pulled it back over him. I didn't want anything too heavy on him, but I didn't want him getting cold either.

Q. Okay.

A. So... I ah... because he wouldn't sleep with his socks on.

Q. Okay.

A. I didn't want him getting cold, so I put that on him.

Q. When you went back up the second time, if you did go up a second time and I'm going to try to maybe name some .... give you some scenarios -- not trying to put anything into your head, but, "Hey, oh yeah, that jogs a memory -- it did happen." Did you cover him back up again?

A. I would have. Yeah. Because he was bad about

35

squirming out from under.

Q. Okay.

A. I would have covered him again.

Q. Did you have to straighten him out in the crib?

A. No. I never had to do that, I would always kiss him.

Q. Okay.

A. Anytime I went into his room, I would kiss him.

Q. Okay. How, and I don't mean this from a housekeeping standpoint, but how picked up is his room normally? Is there stuff stacked on the floor? Is there stuffed toys on the floor?

A. There were blankets laying at the end of his crib, some blankets, and maybe a couple of pillows or something because I would constantly have to change his pillow because his milk would leak out of his bottle and get on the pillows. So, I would keep changing the pillows so I had them there, so I could get to them... and his toys...

Q. Okay. When you changed his pillow, you always had the one right there at the end of his crib?

A. Most of the time they were there.

Q. And we saw some blankets there as well .. if you needed ...

A. Right. They were there ...

Q. If he needed an extra blanket, there were blankets?

A. Yeah.

Q. Okay. Did at 10:30, or any time after 10:30, you go into the closet in his bedroom for any reason?

A. No, not at all.

Q. Okay. Did you at 12 or 12:30, when you went back to check on him, if you did?

A. I'm sure I did.

Q. Was there any need to go into his closet at that time?

A. No... no

Q. When you went up to his room at 10:30, were the closet doors open or closed?

A. They were closed. I always kept the doors closed in his closet.

Q. Always?

A. Unless I had to get something... or go in or out of it.

Q. Did the doors open freely? Was there anything in the way?

A. Oh, no. There's nothing in the way.

Q. How about stuff in the bottom of the closet? My child's stuff falls out of our closet and you have to move stuff to shut the door. Was there any?...

A. No ... There was ... I tried to keep things a little bit neat, you know. It's kinda hard with space. We didn't have that much closet space, but I tried to keep things neat.

Q. What was kept in Joshua's closet?

A. I had blankets... (laughs)... I know ya'll think I had a lot of blankets, but like I said, I'm a cold-natured person. Ah ... blankets and sheets and things were laying on the ah ... like if you looked at the center and looked to this side -- that area was covered with ah ... it might have been stacked just a little bit -- maybe this high.

Q. On the shelf or on the floor?

A. On the floor. I had a sheet or something laying (sic) out there, so it wouldn't actually be on the floor.

Q. Okay.

A. And, I had that stuff stacked there neat and from that point to maybe a little bit further down, any sheets for the beds and pillowcases.

Q. (Magini) This was on the bottom there?

A. On the bottom. On the floor. And, then from there down, I think all that was there -- I had a sewing box in there and we had just ... my daughter had a fish for an aquarium and one of them died about a month ago, and then the other died just last week. I believe and I had never gotten her anymore so I put her ... I cleaned the aquarium out and sit it down in there in that closet. And, then all my clothes and some of Joshua's were hanging in the closet.

Q. Okay.

A. Ahm... all the clothes I had there at the house was in that closet.

Q. Was there a shelf in the closet?

A. Yes, there was s shelf above the clothes that were hanging.

Q. What was on that shelf?

A. Ah... mostly just towels, wash cloths, ahm... on the far end, I had a box...

Q. On the far-right end?

A. Yeah, the far-right hand corner, I had a box that my oldest son that doesn't live with me. He used to like Batman a lot and I had gone to McDonald's when they had the Batman series cup come out and got all the cups and I had them in that box for him so he could have them when I saw him again. And some glasses maybe ... I think there are some glasses in it. It's pretty good sized box. But, it had dividers in it, so nothing got broke. That's why his were in there. I wanted to make sure they were good and protected and make sure nothing got broke.

Q. (Magini) On the right side of the shelf? The far end?

A. On the right side, on the far end. And, Betty Gore, the lady that was with me at the house a while ago, her ah... she had given me one of those big tins of popcorn for Christmas last year and the empty cans were sitting beside that box on that shelf. I think that was all that was in there. Ahm... I can't think of anything else.

Q. Prior to... well, you said you didn't go into his closet at 10:30. When was the last time you went into that closet?

A. I do laundry -- the towels and things. It seems like I put the clothes up... I think I put the towels and things in there... what was last Saturday?... I think it was last Friday. Then I put the towels and wash cloths up on the shelf and I think that was the only time I went in there.

Q. Did Brittany go in the closet?

A. Brittany never went into his room.

Q. Okay.

A. I... I was real big in making sure they had their own rooms. Their own privacy, you know -- this is his room and this is your room... you know...

Q. Okay. When was the last time the closet was opened?

A. It would have had to have been that Friday when I put the towels up.

Q. Okay, (Magini). Do you remember what time it was?

A. It would have been in the afternoon or evening. Because I was in school Friday. It would have been after I got home from there.

Q. Do you smoke?

A. I do smoke.

Q. Ahm... do you smoke in Joshua's room?

A. No.

Q. Okay. At the fire scene...

A. I don't know... wait a minute, now... yeah... I did. You saw a little ashtray in there.

Q. I saw two.

A. I had just gone in there that week and gone through all the clothes in his cabinet and, I had just pulled everything out and I was just sitting there spending an hour or two going through everything and getting things out that he couldn't wear and they were downstairs in a bag and I think they still are.

Q. Okay.

A. Behind the iron... I had an ironing board I was trying to take and see if anybody could use them. I was just trying to get everything situated for winter because it was getting cold and I was changing all the clothes around. So, I had smoked a cigarette in his room that day. (laughs).

Q. Okay. And what day was that?

A. I really don't know. I just... it was ... Let's see. He was sick with a cold most of the week and... let's see; I would probably say maybe Wednesday.

Q. Okay. Was that the last time you smoked in his room?

A. I think that was the only time I smoked in this room. I never spent that much time in his room.

Q. Okay. Why would there have been two ashtrays in his room if you... you know, there is not a lot of smoking in there?

A. I have no idea... I really don't know.

Q. Okay. Joshua was born with a low birth weight.

A. Yeah.

Q. What was Joshua's health prior to the incident?

A. Oh, he was fine. The only thing Josh had was a sinus infection that they were in the process of treating then. I mean, they had just started treating it and all the medicine is still there and, ah... he had allergies ... you know like pollen allergies and that sort of thing, so he had a bottle of Adorax that I would give him. You know, they kept me...They let me have it on hand so if it acted up, I would have it.

Q. Okay.

A. But, other than that, he was fine. He was perfectly healthy.

Q. Okay. Do you drink alcohol?

A. No, I do not. I would occasionally years back. A few years ago, I might would occasionally have a drink, but not... I've never been a drinker.

Q. On this particular night between 10:30 and 12:00 A.M., you had trouble sleeping?

A. Yeah.

Q. Did you take any type of medication at that time?

A. Only what was prescribed. Ah... I recently went to Dr. Allen in Lumberton. He's a neurologist. Three or four weeks ago, I was in my classroom-- In one of my classes, I went blind. I could not see anything. And, so I went to the eye doctor. That was on a Friday. He sent me to a neurologist because he said he thought something might be pressing on my eye -- on the nerves or something. So, he sent me there and he put me on some blood pressure medicine because he felt like it might be a blood flow thing or something that I took in the mornings. And, something at night ahm... I also can't remember what it was for because I was having real bad headaches I think. He thought it might be migraines.

Q. So, did you take two different types of medications that night?

A. Not that night. I just took the one he told me to take at night; I can get it for you.

Q. Is it a sleeping... muscle relaxer?

A. It may be... I don't know if it had anything in it or not. It didn't do anything for me. I don't think it had anything in it -- I don't know. I have never heard of the stuff till he gave it to me.

Q. Did you take any other type of drugs that night?

A. I don't take drugs at all... (laughs) I'm not...

Q. Alright...

A. I'm probably one of the biggest anti-drug people in this County, so...

Q. Steve, I'm sort of at a hold-off right now. Do you have any questions? (Magini) In ah...the closet -- I kinda drew a little diagram as you were explaining... Is this kind of the way things were laid out in that closet? These are the blankets, sheets.... (White) This is the floor.

A. These are pillowcases...

Q. (Magini) Pillowcases, sewing box, the aquarium on the floor, and your clothes and Josh's clothes hanging on hangers?

A. Right.

Q. And up top had some towels and the candy tin -- the

popcorn-- whatever you described.

A. In a box.

Q. In a box?

A. That's about it.

Q. That was it, right? (White). Were there any flammable liquids in the hall that you are aware of?

A. Not that I know of as being flammable.

Q. Okay.

A. There maybe things -- cleaners and things downstairs in the kitchen or something -- bleach and stuff... I don't know.

Q. Okay. When you put Brittany to bed that night around seven, did you hear her other than...?

A. I did not hear her. I remember when I went and looked at him when he called out and I looked in on her and she was laying on her back sound asleep peaceful like always and I pulled her sheet up over her.

Q. Okay. Was she laying in her bed?

A. She was on her bed.

Q. (Magini) You mentioned earlier that the cord from the heater downstairs was warm. Now, was that heater plugged into an extension cord?

A. It was. But, it was a brand-new extension cord we had just got that week when they started calling for cold weather.

Q. Now, was that extension cord what was warm or was it the cord from the heater?

A. It was the cord from the heater. Well, actually both of them. I believe I felt both of them.

Q. Both of them?

A. And it was just warm. Yeah, because I remember saying the cord was a new cord, so it shouldn't have been like that.

Q. Okay. Now, this was a small ah... household interior extension cord.

A. Yeah. What other kind is there? (Laughs)

Q. Well, they have a heavy duty...

A. Oh, well I thought those were.

Q. (Magini) Well, let's see. When Josh cried out about 10:30 or so and you left to check on him with a flashlight, were you smoking at the time? Do you remember?

A. I doubt it. No... I didn't smoke that much at night and in the evenings. I was more in the mornings with coffee.

Q. (White) Would it be normal for you if you couldn't sleep, to light up a cigarette?

A. I probably would have when I was sitting there reading, yeah.

Q. Okay. Could you have possibly, when he cried out, still had a cigarette in your mouth and then went up?

A. Certainly not... first, I can't do that. I have never understood how people can have a cigarette in their mouth and walk around with it, but I... had the flashlight in my right hand when I went up to check on him and used my left hand to do everything else, so there's... certainly not...

Q. (Magini) Okay. Now, when you went upstairs the first time after Brittany had called out and you realized that there was a fire upstairs, you were able to get up the stairs into the hallway?

A. I was actually able to get as far to his door and that's when it came over me.

Q. Right to his door?

A. Right at his door.

Q. And when you got to his door, you could see it coming out of his closet?

A. Oh, I could see it, I could feel it, I could hear it -- I could do it all, I mean...

Q. And it seemed to be coming from your left in the closet?

A. Yeah.

Q. And, then it came over your head?

Justice for Baby Josh

A. Yeah.

Q. Alright.

A. It's like all of a sudden when I got there -- It was just like -- it was well, she's here, let's get her. It's kind of the way I have to look at it now, you know, okay, there's somebody else. Let's get 'em. And, it comes at me just like that... it was just...

Q. Okay. Now, were you standing or were you...?

A. Probably half and half. I couldn't stand all the way up because it was hot and it was smoking up. And, I was trying to stay down below the smoke so I could get into him. And then, by the time I turned around to go to her, it's like it just consumed everything upstairs. The smoke was just everywhere -- up, down, everywhere. No matter how you went, it was there.

Q. Now... ah... did you notice the door to Joshua's room; was it still open?

A. Yeah... when I went... the first time I went up. I didn't even notice the second time. I don't even think I could see it the second time.

Q. Okay.

A. I'm trying to remember... and I don't. I know the first time it was there. I know it was there.

Q. Okay. Now, could you see... could you see the flames coming across the ceiling? I don't want to put words in your mouth, but...

A. No, I can't say if I did or not. I really don't remember.

Q. Was it a glow or were you able to see...?

A. It was just coming out. It was like shooting out... flames. Just shooting out real far...

Q. Okay.

A.   Ahm... But when I heard the "whoosh" sound, then it went across the ceiling. It was like every ceiling up there was like at one time... It went up at one time. It just come over me.

Q.   Okay.

A.   Somebody... Betty's boyfriend just recently stopped working with the fire department. He worked with them for years and he called that something I don't remember what it was...

Q.   Flash-over?

A.   Yeah, that's what it was.

Q.   I guess it's a matter of semantics, but more like a rollover.

A.   Well, that's true... it kinda, you know, that kind of...

Q.   It just rolled right out...

A.   It's such a weird sound.

Q.   (White) When you decided to go to bed that night, is it customary for you to put on night clothes versus jeans and a shirt? What did...?

A.   Well, it depends...

Q.   What did you have on?

A.   I mean, it's like I said. I just got tired and just laid down.

Q.   What did you have on that night when you laid down on the sofa to go to sleep?

A.   I think I had this on. I think this is the very clothes I got on now. And, my shoes were beside the couch, and I honestly don't know how I got my shoes or my glasses or any of that... I don't know how I got that stuff.

Q.   Did you have those on when you wound up outside?

A.   Somehow. I think. I'm assuming I did. I don't know why anybody else would get them and bring them to me or anything.

Q.   So, when you wound up outside, you were fully clothed?

A. Yeah, unless I... I mean the only thing... that's been going through my mind ever since -- I don't know how I got my shoes on unless I didn't have any shoes on... off to start with. I just don't remember.

Q. Okay, when you were at...

A. I know... I do normally put a gown on. I normally put... I have a jump suit-like thing that you sleep in that I sometimes wear.

Q. Okay. When you go to the top of the stairs and you couldn't get into Josh's room, when was the second time that you actually heard Brittany call your name or call "Mommy"?

A. I think it was between the time I came down and got the phone. I think I was yelling up to her and talking to them at the same time and trying to tell her I was there and trying to get her down. I told her to come down -- come downstairs. I think. I want to say it was about the same time.

Q. Okay. You earlier mentioned that the first time you were up there, you couldn't get into Josh's room, but you went into Brittany's room...

A. I tried to... but is was so black, I couldn't see her. I was trying to feel her... I couldn't get to her. I couldn't find her...

Q. So, did you get into her room?

A. No. It was all happening so quick. It was like it just come out and I couldn't breathe. I couldn't breathe at all. I forgot the "get down low" thing. I just totally forgot it.

Q. So, you didn't actually get into Brittany's room?

A. No, I couldn't get in her room.

Q. Couldn't feel any bed or...

A. I couldn't see her. I couldn't hear her anymore; I couldn't... I knew she was there; I just couldn't figure out where?

Q. So, then you went downstairs and made the call, but then you heard her again?

46

Justice for Baby Josh

A. Right.

Q. Okay. Didn't you hear her screaming or crying or anything when you were up there?

A. Not in between...

Q. Okay.

A. I mean, I never heard her. If I did, I didn't... I don't know...

Q. Didn't register?

A. I don't know. My mind was trying to get to where the fire was at ... getting him out and then get her and get us. It was like ... because I knew he was the one in immediate danger. I knew it was in his room.

Q. Okay.

A. And I think I was pushing there and yelling at the same time for her to get out because I thought she'd be able to, I mean, her being older and you know, she knew to go downstairs. And the only thing I could think of was that Brittany might have been on the other side of her bed and just couldn't get ... was scared to come across or something. I don't know ... I don't know.

Q. Okay. Describe for me how you met Rodney.

A. (Laughs) Well, actually he said I met him when I was a kid. I don't remember it. But, we were at school. He began classes in criminal justice last spring. I think,'95'. We just talked and ended up together. I don't know how to put it.

Q. Okay. Were you living at 101 Wall Street permanent? Had you pretty much moved in there? Is that your permanent residence?

A. No, this is my residence. But I was there. I probably spent more time there than here.

Q. When did you decide to -- quote unquote -- move in with Rodney?

A. I hadn't really... we had actually talked about the last couple of weeks about going and moving... finding a one-story place and ahm... maybe moving in then... I had seen

47

something in the paper about a house for sale.

Q. How many bedrooms did that house have that you saw for sale?

A. I think it was three. I'm pretty sure because it was something that was in the paper -- I think last Tuesday's paper. It had four acres of land or something with it and we were planning on opening a kennel up and ahm...

Q. When was it that you decided... that... when did you and Rodney start spending time together overnight?

A. Oh gosh!... that was a long time ago. I was in the apartments, then. I lived in some apartments over in Tabor Villa.

Q. Okay.

A. And he would come over occasionally and spend the night.

Q. Okay. When did you start leaving the kids clothes? You mentioned that the closet had some of yours and Joshua's clothes in it and we noticed several toys while we were there.

A. I don't remember. I really don't remember.

Q. How would you describe your relationship with Rodney?

A. It was the best, I mean, (laughs) we had plans to get married. Ahm... or have plans to get married.

Q. Are you currently engaged or...?

A. I don't know if I want to call it that or not. I just... we just talked about it and we were gonna do it. And, he had planned to adopt both kids and...

Q. Had you set a date to get married?

A. I did. I don't know if he did or not... (laughs). I told him he better be there... (laughs).

Q. When was the date?

A. The last of July of next year...

Q. Of '97?

A. Yeah. Last Sunday of July. I can't remember the

exact date, but I remember the last Sunday in July.

Q. Okay. So, you describe your relationship as the best? You had a good relationship?

A. Oh, yeah.

Q. You mentioned that he was going to adopt the two kids. Tell me about your other... you mentioned three other kids. Tell me about your three other children.

A. Ahm... what do you want to know, I mean... there's a lot I can tell you. I don't know...

Q. Okay. I guess...

A. You want to know why I don't have them?

Q. Well, why are they not living with you, their ages -- that kind of thing?

A. Ah... well, I guess the best way to start is my ex-husband was in the military and he got kicked out. And, at the same time, he was told that I found out he had been running around on me for three years. And, ah ... so I told him he could come here and stay. We were going to move in with Mom. But, he had to ... but as soon as he got a job, he was going to move out. And, ah ... he agreed to that. As far as the marriage, actually it had ended. He was here to get himself straightened out and then he had to leave.

Q. How many times have you been married?

A. One.

Q. Are all...?

A. No. They are not all the same kids from all the same dads.

Q. How about the three that are not with you? Do they have the same father?

A. That was Brian's. That was my ex-husband.

Q. Okay. Are the children with him now?

A. No.

Q. Okay. Where are those children now?

A. He's the one, I think that was the biggest thing to causing them to be adopted. He ah ... I don't think he wanted to pay child support.

Q. Were they taken away from you? I mean, describe for me... did you decide to put them up for adoption?

A. I'll be honest with you. I have a lot of unanswered questions with that. Because, I don't know. Mom might be able to help me. But I know that I had talked to her about it after Brian had finally moved out. My brother had just died. He had been killed from an alcohol related accident. And, I couldn't... that's one reason I am anti-alcohol... when I saw what happened, but we ah... (speaks to her mother in background -- "I'll be in here in a little while.") Anyway, he died and then Brian left and I had no job and no training and my car was broken down. But, I finally got it fixed and told Mom I was going to go to Charlotte and try to get a job and get straightened out where I could take care of the kids. And, she agreed to keep them here and actually help take care of them and I would visit them and whatever for however long it took. I got there and got a job and everything was fine and the next thing I know, I got a call saying I had to put my kids up for adoption. I don't know exactly what happened.

Q. Who was that call from?

A. Mom.

Q. Okay.

A. And ah... I talked to... I know that ...

Q. Was Social Services involved?

A. Social Services was involved somehow. And, I remember I just didn't have the money for a lawyer. I couldn't fight anybody on anything. I didn't know what to do or how to do... I didn't know...

Q. Who would you have been fighting?

A. I think it would have been my ex-husband. I think he's who did all of it.

Q. Was he seeking custody of the kids?

A. No, he just didn't want anything to do with them. I don't think he wanted to part with the money.

Q. Why?

A. Because he was having to pay a high child support that he never did pay...

Q. Okay.

A. I don't know. Something strange happened to my ex-husband. He wasn't like that...

Q. How old were you when you had your first child?

A. Eighteen... I was almost 19. I was... he was born in February and I turned 19 in May.

Q. Where do those children live now?

A. Ah... Bradley... my oldest one is in Kentucky. Ashley, the one next to -- under him. She lived in Whiteville when all this happened and then ah... her adopted father was a highway patrolman and they transferred him and I don't know where they are at. I know they are somewhere in North Carolina -- I just don't know where; and, then Timmy -- he's just outside of town here. Little Timmy is just right here.

Q. Okay. Those three did not have the same father as Joshua and Brittany?

A. No, and Joshua's and Brittany's father is not the same.

Q. Okay.

A. I know this sounds bad, but...

Q. Well... no... Hey!... no judgment of anything...

A. I just made some wrong choices.

Q. Were you married to Joshua's or Brittany's father?

A. No.

Q. Okay. Do Joshua's... did... does... do you know who Joshua's father is?

A. On, yeah.

Q. Okay. Is he in town locally?

A. No.

Q. Where is he?

A. He's in Hallsboro.

Q. Where is Hallsboro? Is that in North Carolina?

A   Yeah. It's just outside of Whiteville.

Q.   Does ah... Joshua's father pay child support?

A.   He... I was getting help from the State... AFDC and all and they had just ordered a paternity test because he demanded it and we just got the results back showing it was his and he had been told he had to start to do something.

Q.   When did all this take place?

A.   That was in the last two or three weeks. Just in the last few weeks.

Q.   Had you seen Joshua's father recently?

A.   The only time was the day we went and did the blood test.

Q.   And how long was that... two or three weeks?

A.   Now, the blood test was done ... first part of September, I think. Somewhere in September, I think because they told me it would take 4-6 weeks to get it back, and it was right at four weeks when I got it back ... So, it has been at least ...

Q.   So, did Joshua's father disclaim him as being his child?

A.   When I called him and told him Joshua had been born, I asked him -- I said, "Do you want your name on the birth certificate?" and he said, "Naw, I don't want anything to do with it?" So, everything was left in my name, so he had my name. And, that was just fine, you know. I told everybody I never held it against Kenny. It was just simply his belief that it was not right to bring a child into the world the way it is. He did not want any children at all. And, it was just an accident.

Q.   What is Kenny's full name?

A.   Kenneth. I think it's Bryant...

Q.   Okay. Do you know his address or phone number?

A.   His address is (deleted), but I don't know the number. He lives with his mother and step-father. Their last name is (deleted).

Q.   Okay. How old is... Kenny? Is that his name?

A.   I think he's the same age as I am. He's either 31 or 32. I think he's 32.

Q.   Okay.

A.   I know his birthday is on January 1st.

Q.   Okay.

A.   I remember it being New Years.

Q.   Had there been a bitter dispute over this issue on whether or not Kenny was the father of Joshua?

A.   No. I mean, I knew it and he knew it... it was just -- I really don't think he was the one who demanded the blood test. I think it was his mom. His mom really freaked over this. She was bad on us, I mean really bad.

Q.   Did you wish... I mean... you obviously went to court over the paternal thing.

A.   No. We never went to court.

Q.   Why the issue of the blood test?

A.   Because I was getting help from the State and they had ordered him to pay child support to help repay the State and to help me out and I told them to just leave him alone, you know, if he didn't want to... I'm not going to force somebody to do something for their child.

Q.   So, you are not forcing that?

A.   Oh, no. I was... by no means -- I was not forcing that. I told them not to, but they had to do what they had to do.

Q.   So, Kenny didn't have anything to do with Josh?

A.   No. He has never seen him. He never saw him -- never had a picture of him or nothing.

Q.   Okay. Had you been trying to get Kenny to take Joshua?

A.   Absolutely not!

Q.   Had you been trying to have Kenny adopt to go and live with him?

A.   Oh, no. Now, when I had him, they told me at the

hospital that they needed information on his background, so I
had to call his Mama and just assumed Kenny had told his
Mama by this point that I had just had her grandchild. And, I
learned real quick that he hadn't told her anything and she
was real angry.

Q. At you?

A. At me. At him. At everybody for not saying
anything and she had that right. But, I assumed that he had
told her. But then when I got home, you know -- I would
come back and forth from this apartment to the hospital and
I... on one of the trips home, she called and wanted to go see
him, and I told her that would be fine, but I had to be there
because I knew she was angry and I didn't want her there by
herself. So... he was in a nursery or whatever. When I said
she couldn't go, she said, "Well, I'm going to take you to
court and I'm going to get custody of him. And, I told her,
"You are not going to do it because it's my child and there's
no reason. And, she tried to pull in the stuff about my other
three kids and my mom told her real quick that was not my
fault. That was something that should never have happened.
Ahm... as far as adoption goes, she was determined she was
going to and then I never heard nothing from neither of them.
It's like all of sudden they just shut up and I never heard
nothing from any of them.

Q. Was Joshua up for adoption?

A. No. Absolutely not...

Q. Has he ever been up for adoption?

A. No, no... That was... ya'll have to understand. I think
when these other three left me, I was trying to replace them,
and, I wanted that little boy more than anything in this world.

Q. I understand.

A. I remember when I had him and they done
ultrasounds and they told me it was a boy and I was so happy.
But, when I went to have him and he was born, the doctor,
out of a joke, said, "I believe it's a girl," and I didn't really

54

react, I don't think. And then she looked over at me and said, "I'm just joking; you've got a boy." I remember that, you know, her trying to pull that little ah... (laughs), but I think I was trying to get them back, and...

Q. Had there been any recent activities... Had Joshua not been put up for adoption?

A. No.

Q. Had there been any recent activities where the State or Social Services or anyone else was trying to take Joshua from you?

A. The only incident that ever happened was so stupid it was pathetic, but ah... and you can certainly check it. This was really stupid -- when he was a little baby. I can't remember how old he was -- he was very young. He was on a... monitor. I don't know if you know what that is or not...

Q. No, I don't...

A. Well, they had him on for his weight being so low, they were scared. It was more of a precautionary measure. But, it was done for babies that stop breathing in their sleep or something. It alarms... so, it had to stay on 24 hours a day. And, at that point, I was the only one who knew CPR and I wouldn't let him be with anybody. I think that's how he ended up going with me everywhere now... I kept that there... you know, he stayed with me, and, ah... so I had to go to school for something and I don't remember exactly what because it was in the middle of a quarter when I had him and I remember I had to do papers to keep that going and ah... a friend... if you want to call her a friend. I don't know what to call them, but her name is Tammy White. She ah... she had seen me with the baby and she had seen me leave the school going to the parking lot with him. It was a real hot day; and, my car was parked next to another girl's car that was a student in my class and she was a nurse. She had been a nurse for about 20 years, I think, and had dealt with kids. I told her -- I said, "Joy, I forgot; I need to call Mom." So, I went back to call Mom. So, I went and she kept him with her. And, I went back and called Mom. And, when the time -- just a few minutes, I come out and there were cops there. Everybody's there. And Tammy had apparently thought that I had left him in the car in the heat. So, she reported it to everybody. So, yeah, there was some kind of investigation, but it was easily cleared up.

Q. How long ago was that?

A. Well, he was born in May. I would say it was probably in June, maybe. It was not long after...

Q. Nothing in the last couple of months as far as the State or Social Services to take Josh away from you?

A. No, not at all...

Q. Okay. And from nowhere else either?

A. Not that I...

Q. (Magini) Terry, the house, it's an older house?

A. Yeah, it was.

Q. And the outlets... There aren't as many outlets as you would have in a new house...

A. Right.

Q. Did you have any problem ahm... functioning in the house that way? I mean, as far as appliances and that sort of thing?

A. Well, I ah... sort of... kinda... well, it wasn't really a problem because I got the little surge protector things where you could plug more than just one thing in an outlet. I mean... if I needed more than one thing in a room, then I would use those.

Q. Have you ever had to replace any of the fuses in the fuse box?

A. Rodney replaced something... one or two when he first moved in there, but as far as I know, there is nothing other than that.

Q. Nothing since?

A. No.

Q. And this is going back to May?

A. May 1st. It was rented.

Q. Had you just been running the heaters?

A. The only thing I know of that was abnormal lately was when Fran hit... Well, when we moved in, Mike told him he was going to redo the roof anyway because ah ... the shingles -- well, it just looked like a rough roof and it needed work. He hadn't done that when Fran come in and apparently, Fran took some shingles off the roof... well, they were because I picked them up... a lot of people did. Everybody was picking up shingles. Ah... There was a leak in Joshua's room about halfway to his crib from the door. And, ah... It had started bowing... the water. Every time it has rained since Fran, it has caused more bowing.

Q. (Matt). You said about halfway... Would that have been... Would that have been the light fixture?

A. There is some kind of beam or something... yeah, I believe there is a light fixture in front of it... like right straight in front where the bow was at. And, ah... nobody -- He told Mr. Wright, the other owner about it right after Fran hit. He told them there was a leak in the room and he told him he would get somebody on it to look at it and nobody ever came until last week. I can't remember what day... We just happened to be there. Joshua was sick and I didn't want to take him to school -- day care and all and ah... we just happened to be there and this guy came and checked things out and he... I told him there has got to be water getting up in that attic because wood don't bow like that for no reason... and ah... it leaking and all... that was the only thing abnormal and all... then the lights started flickering every now and then downstairs. You would notice. In the last week or so, I would notice they would flicker every now and then.

Q. (Magini) Which lights downstairs?

A. Ah... the overhead light. I didn't use it much, but when it was on... or whatever. It would flicker... and ah... the kitchen.

Q. The kitchen? Which light in the kitchen, now?

A. The overhead... There are two lights in there. Both of those would flicker. That was in the last week or so... I think it's been in the last week. I don't even know what day it is right now.

Q. Now ah... This is in the last week, you say?

A. It hadn't been too long... since I noticed all this starting.

Q. Now has this been since you have had the heaters -- the heater plugged in?

A. That heater was not used unless it got cold. I haven't had them that long. In fact, they are Mom's. I took them down there from here. In fact, she's got one just like them here in her room. And... ah... we were kind of debating did we want to move out of there into another house or maybe get gas or something. Because I just didn't like the idea of baseboard heat. I didn't trust it. It was sort of stupid. Maybe I should've, I don't know. It seems like the harder I try, the worst things get...

Q. I really can't think of anything else, Matt. (Matt) I think I have pretty much covered everything I wanted to cover. Ahm... Terry, is there anything that we have not asked you about that maybe you would like to mention or note?

A. I'm kinda wondering why everyone is asking me about my other three kids. I don't understand what's bringing them into this.

Q. The only reason I asked you is I need to find out who is related to you. Who has an interest -- that type of thing. What went on.

A. I was just curious...

Q. I don't think...

A. It just seems like...

Q. The police department may have also mentioned it. I

don't know.

A. I mean, I have had counseling with it and they have all told me the only thing I can do is wait until they get old enough and I can talk to them and tell them what happened...

Q. What did happen? You mentioned that it was kinda one of those things.

A. I don't know... I just don't know. I just know that one day I had them and one day I didn't.

Q. Okay.

A. And, I was never told that I could go back a year later and get them -- up to a year later. I didn't know any of that. That's one reason I went into this field... into criminal justice. I wanted to know the laws.

Q. Going back to Saturday night -- between 10:30 and the time the fire occurred, you are absolutely certain that Joshua's closet door was closed?

A. Yep.

Q. You are absolutely certain that you didn't have to go into that closet whether it be to get a blanket or to put some...

A. Absolutely not.

Q. More towels away?

A. Absolutely not!

Q. You didn't go into the closet at all?

A. When they went to bed, I tried not to go into their rooms.

Q. Sure.

A. Because, I mean... they were light sleepers... I just tried not to go into their rooms, but when he cried naturally, I went in and... that was the only time -- you know, if he cried out, I went...

Q. Okay, are you absolutely...?

A. And that's why the doors were open to their rooms... because I never believed in closing doors to my kid's rooms so I could hear them.

Q. Okay, are you absolutely certain that you didn't

59

carry a cigarette up to his room?

A.   I know I didn't... I know I didn't... ah... I had just put my desk... It had been upstairs and I had put it up in the bedroom and if I walked up there, I might smoke in my room... But, I hadn't done that... in I don't know when.

Q.   None of that would have been put in Joshua's closet?

A.   Oh, certainly not and ah... Mike had somebody to come and paint the house and he had some empty cans out back and I think Rodney moved them finally and I'm not sure if he did or not.

Q.   Okay.

A.   But no, there is none of that stuff.

Q.   Are there any electrical appliances in the closet?

A.   No, nothing... oh, I take that back. There was ah... there might have been a humidifier that I had in his room. If I needed it, it was there, but I hadn't used it in such a long time.

Q.   Was it plugged in?

A.   Oh, certainly not. If it was there in that room, it was on the shelf on top; but, I really can't remember if it was there or not. That's the only thing I can think of that would have been in his room.

Q.   Anything else?

(Magini). No, I have nothing.

(White). Terry, did you understand all the questions asked you?

A.   Yeah.

Q.   Were your answers true to the best of your knowledge?

A.   Yeah.

Q.   Okay. And this is Matt White concluding my recorded statement with Ms. Hinson. Again, today's date is October 22, 1996. Approximate time is 5:20 P.M. Concluding with me is Mr. Steve Magini. Ms. Hinson, with your permission, I will stop my recorder.

    A.   Okay.

The 101 Wall Street Property

    On October 23, 1996, and again on November 1, SBI Agent Matt White conducts a phone interview with Mike Jones, who tells Agent White that he and Attorney Richard Wright, partners in Wall Street Investment Company, have owned the 101 Wall St. property about 20 years. Jones tells White he believes the house was built around 1940. Ms. Emma Smith was the original owner. Jones and his partner, attorney Richard Wright, bought the property from Ms. Smith, through their partnership in Wall Street Investment. The property is insured by US F&G for $30,000. An adjuster had gone to assess minor roof damage sustained by Hurricane Fran (September 5, 1996). Jones recalls no other claims. He says the property is currently leased to Rodney Strickland, who put ditto marks under the name Strickland and beside the first name of Terri to make it appear that she is Terri Strickland instead of Terri Hinson. The lease began in May of 1996. Jones explains that Rodney had agreed to repair a kitchen faucet, reinstall a stairway post and banister, and paint the interior with paint and materials furnished by the lessor.

    Jones maintains there have been no problems reported to him as to the condition of the property and if there have been complaints from renters, they have been minor.

    A policeman by the name of Brian Ramey had been the previous tenant from April 10, 1995, or for about a year before Strickland's lease began.

    To the best of his knowledge, Jones says there have been no electrical problems in the house. He does recall that Hurricane Fran (June, 1996), blew off a few shingles, but not enough to produce any leaking and none was ever reported by the Strickland tenants.

He also tells Agent White that the Stricklands never reported any electrical problems, nor did they ever request smoke detectors. Jones did not know whether there were smoke detectors in the house or if there recently had been and they'd been removed.

If there had been any additions, alterations, or changes in light fixtures, they would have been made "several years ago."

Jones concludes by mentioning that the man he hired to repair the kitchen faucet two months ago, was also an electrician, who could have fixed any electrical problems which the Stricklands brought to his attention.

STATEMENT OF ATF CERTIFIED FIRE INVESTIGATOR

To: Special Agent in Charge
Date: October 24, 1996

This report relates to the examination of a structure fire at 101 Wall Street, Tabor City, North Carolina, 28463. The fire took place on October 20, 1996, at about 3:57 A.M. The examination took place on October 20, 1996, and October 22, 1996.

Synopsis of Incident
On Sunday, October 20, 1996, at approximately 3:57 A.M., a fire was reported to the Columbus County 911 Center. The location of the fire was 101 Wall Street, Tabor City, North Carolina. The structure is a single family, a two-story home which was involved in fire when the Tabor City Volunteer Fire Department arrived.

The resident, Terri Hinson, was present at the time of

the fire. Two of Hinson's children were also present, Joshua Hinson, 17 months old, and his sister, Brittany Hinson, 4 years old. Terri Hinson escaped the structure, Brittany and Joshua were rescued by firefighters. Joshua was later pronounced dead at Loris Community Hospital. Brittany was airlifted to the University of South Carolina at Charleston Medical Center. Fire Chief Jerry Watts and Police Chief Robert Wooster requested the assistance of the State Bureau of Investigation and subsequently ATF in determining the origin and cause of the fire.

Participating Fire Investigators

An examination of the scene was initially conducted by North Carolina State Bureau of Investigation Special Agent Matt White on October 20, 1996, under a North Carolina District Court Search Warrant. On October 22, 1996, Special Agent White and ATF Special Agent Frank Malter jointly examined the scene with consent and participation of Terri Hinson.

Witness Reports

Witness reports revealed the fire was called into the Columbus County 911 Center at 3:57 A.M. by Terri Hinson. The Tabor City Police and Fire Departments were dispatched at 3:57 A.M. First arriving police officers observed smoke emanating from the gable on the second floor of the house. Police Officer Robert Moyer made an attempt to rescue the children by entering the front door and going upstairs. Near the top of the stairs, Moyer experienced heavy smoke and some heat, and returned to the first-floor living room area where he was met by Hinson and Police Officer Russell. Moyer and Russell exited the house and checked the perimeter. In the rear of the house, they observed flames projecting through the roof in the vent pipe.

First responding firefighters found smoke emanating

from the gable vent of the attic facing Wall Street. Firefighters entered the house after being appraised of the location of the children. The first firefighter entered the front door, ascended the stairs and entered the first bedroom on the left, where he located Brittany on the floor and removed her from the house. Firefighter Jeff Graham (should be Fowler) passed the first firefighter exiting with Brittany. Graham (Fowler) entered the house and ascended the stairs. Graham (Fowler) searched Brittany's bedroom and then searched the third bedroom, Terri Hinson's. After completing searches of these bedrooms, Graham (Fowler) entered Josh's bedroom and located and removed him from the crib and exited the premises.

The house is jointly owned by Michael Jones and Richard Wright. The structure was insured by U.S. F&G for $30,000. The house is rented by Rodney Strickland with Terri Hinson and the children listed as tenants under the last name of Strickland. The house was rented by Strickland in May of 1996.

Building Construction

The house is a two-story, three bedrooms, wood frame structure with brick veneer on the first floor and wood clapboard covering the exterior of the second floor. The structure is about 55 years old. The roof is "A"-framed, tongue and grove pine boards covered with tar paper and asphalt roofing shingles. The second-floor ceiling and walls were constructed of wood frame, covered with painted tongue and groove boards.

Scene Examination

Assistance in the cause and origin determination was requested by the Tabor City Police and Fire Departments. An exterior examination of the scene disclosed the only fire damage was a hole burned through the roof in the area of the vent pipe. Heavy smoke soot from the gable vents and between the wood clapboards covering the second floor was also observed. The first floor consisted of a living room, kitchen, and laundry area. Light smoke and water damage were observed throughout the first floor. Paint blistering from the heat of the fire was observed on the landing area of the second floor. No fire damage was observed outside Joshua's bedroom, the room of origin. The hollow-framed bedroom door was open at the time of the fire and about one foot of the wood veneer was burned away at the top. On the far-right wall was the crib the victim was recovered from. The crib sustained radiant heat damage and no direct flame contact. The chest of drawers located on the back wall, between the two windows, received only radiant heat damage to the side exposed to the closet. The ceiling exhibited fire damage approximately three feet from the double door closet located on the left side of the room. The floor covering exhibited a circular burn pattern consistent with the right closet door. The interior of the closet exhibited the greatest fire damage to include a hole which burned through the tongue and groove ceiling, ceiling joist, and roof of the house.

One electrical outlet was located in the closet wall away from the area of origin. The outlet box was metal and had nothing plugged into it. Examination of the outlet box and conductors did not reveal any internal heating.

A painted wood shelf extended the length of the closet above the level of the electrical outlet and metal closet rod. Examination of the closet shelf revealed the heaviest burning on the underside. No accidental ignition source was located within the right-side area of the closet.

Conclusion

The area of origin of the fire was determined to be the closet of Joshua's bedroom. The point of origin was the right side of the center below the closet shelf. All accidental causes in the area of origin were eliminated. This was an incendiary fire, intentionally started by a person or persons unknown.

Number of Fatalities and/or Injuries
Fatalities -- Hinson, Joshua Cade, W/M, Date of birth, May 10, 1995
Injuries --   Hinson, Brittany W/F, Date of birth, September 10, 1992

Interview of Terri Hinson by Department of Social Services Case Worker Jennifer Baldwin on October 24, 1996

Social Services worker Jennifer Baldwin makes a home visit to Terri Hinson's residence in Fair Bluff, NC, where she learns from Terri's brother, Harry Hinson, that Terri and her mom have gone to Tabor City to "try to get some stuff out," after which they will be leaving for Charleston. Baldwin leaves a reply message, before driving to Tabor City.

Upon arriving at the place of the fire, Baldwin finds Terri Hinson, Terri's mother Bernice Prince, and Rodney Strickland.

Baldwin tells Terri Hinson that DSS has received a referral on Brittany. The mother becomes "very upset," claiming she has been questioned by "everyone." She says, "what's there to investigate; he's gone and nothing is going to bring my baby back. I can't grieve for people wanting to ask questions." Hinson becomes tearful. She tells Baldwin to make the interview brief because she's trying to get to her daughter in Charleston. (Brittany was airlifted 4 days ago.)

Mr. Strickland approaches telling Baldwin it might be better to do the interview later.

Ms. Hinson says she wants to get it over with. When

asked about the events the night of October 20, Ms. Hinson relates that her mom had kept Brittany for a couple of hours that day and would come over later so Ms. Hinson could fix her mother's hair.

Ms. Hinson plugged the curling iron into an extension cord downstairs in the living room. Hinson notices the extension cord is hot, and that since Hurricane Fran there has been a lot of damage to the house, and that she has been afraid that the water "damage could cause some kind of electrical problem." Hinson tells DSS case worker Baldwin that because the heater "might catch on fire," she slept downstairs "just in case anything happened."

Hinson says she had trouble sleeping that night. She had been working on a paper for college and had been reading a lot of newspapers her mother had saved for her. She had fallen asleep when she heard Brittany cry out, "I'm scared," and when Ms. Hinson "looked up," she could see "a red and orange glow from upstairs." She then ran upstairs. "Josh's door was open." She started across the doorway and "flames blew out at her." She heard Joshua say "Momma" twice," and also heard "Brittany twice." Ms. Hinson yelled to Brittany "to listen to her voice." She was telling Brittany to go downstairs. She claims she could not see Brittany. Ms. Hinson tells Baldwin, she then ran downstairs, got her cordless phone, and called 911, and then went back upstairs with the phone in her hand, but could not get to the top step because of the fire.

Baldwin and Hinson now enter the burned residence. Ms. Hinson points to the extension cord which she thought was hot. Baldwin observes the extension cord lying across the opening of the door. The couch is on the far-right side of the room, the stairs on the left, and extensive water damage to the ceiling. Ms. Hinson tells Baldwin she was laying on the couch with her head facing away from the door.

Baldwin and Hinson go upstairs, where Baldwin notes

that Joshua's room is directly in front of the stairs. Ms. Hinson's room is to the right and Brittany's room to the left, but cater-corner to the stairs. Joshua's room is severely burned.

Ms. Hinson recounts that when she heard Brittany cry out, she ran up the stairs, mid-way up the stairs she heard Joshua cry "Momma," heard him again as she got to the top of the stairs, that when she got to Joshua's door, she heard a noise that sounded like a "woosh," and that "fire flew out at me." Ms. Hinson tells DSS case worker, she "did not hear Joshua anymore." Next, she turned around and went to Brittany's door, calling out to her and telling Brittany to come to her. Ms. Hinson maintains she was crouched down, but because it was "smokey and black," she could not see, nor did she hear Brittany. Ms. Hinson, reports having trouble breathing. She went downstairs and got the cordless phone, went back upstairs with the phone, but could not get to the top because of the smoke and fire. She may have heard Brittany while she was on the phone and while she was yelling for Brittany to come to her. Ms. Hinson heard the police arrive and headed downstairs where she met them. She claims one officer went upstairs and she was following him when the other officer told her to come back downstairs. The officer who went up could not get to Brittany.

The firefighters "got there right after the police." She was told by Tracey Fowler "got Brittany," but doesn't how "they got Josh out."

She says the police told her the fire started in the closet, where she says, she had her clothes hanging and some sheets on the floor.

Hinson and Baldwin enter Josh's room, which is "badly burned." The closet is "on the left wall with the crib on the right. Ms. Hinson faces the closet but does not turn in the direction of the crib. She did point to the bowed area in the ceiling which she claims was caused by water damage from Hurricane Fran. When Baldwin said she could see two bowed areas, Ms. Hinson claimed that before the fire there was only one – the one closest to the inner wall.

DSS case worker Baldwin and Ms. Hinson proceed to Brittany's room, where Baldwin notes smoke and water damage. Ms. Hinson says from what she had been told, Brittany was found lying "beside the window."

Back outside, Baldwin asks Ms. Hinson if she is aware of any injuries Brittany had sustained. Baldwin adds she had heard Brittany was not breathing when they first found her, but that she was revived on the way to the hospital, where they noticed a burn on her heel the size of a quarter, for which Ms. Hinson explains must have occurred "while they were taking her out."

When Baldwin reminds Ms. Hinson that Hinson was reported to have had her clothes on, including her shoes, Hinson answers she doesn't know when she put them on but did recall that when she arrived at the hospital, she had her shoes on.

Ms. Hinson says to Baldwin, "It might sound crazy, but Brittany knew it was going to happen. Two weeks ago, Brittany ran down the stairs, saying, "Momma, Jesus is here – outside the window." Brittany told me to tell grandma to bring two ladders so she and Josh can get out. She was trying to tell me something, but I didn't listen. I will from now on."

Baldwin asked Ms. Hinson if she had left any lights on when she fell asleep the night of the fire. Hinson said there was one light on top of the entertainment center, but it was not on when she awoke the night of the fire. Ms. Hinson did say there was a clock in her room. Baldwin and Hinson go upstairs into Hinson's bedroom. The clock read 3:57 or 3:58. Ms. Hinson says the clock could not be right if the electricity had already gone off, "because the light downstairs was off. Somebody has messed with that clock." Ms. Hinson says she sees what is happening. "Somebody is trying to set me up."

She didn't understand why they were investigating "what killed my baby. I know what killed my baby– Hurricane Fran. No investigation is going to bring my baby back. Somebody is trying to pin it on me. They've got to make somebody responsible. Richard Wright and Mike Jones own the house and I contacted them about problems with water damage. They are trying to pin it on me because they don't want to have to pay for my baby. I don't want nothing from them."

When Baldwin asks Ms. Hinson if she thought she was a suspect, Ms. Hinson replies that the Tabor City Police Chief said it was a set fire, but that when she talked to the SBI, they didn't act like anything was wrong. She told them about the water damage and they went through the house with her.

Baldwin asks Ms. Hinson if she knew of anyone who would have set the fire, to which Ms. Hinson stated that Brittany's father was the only one, but he didn't have the opportunity. She added the Police Chief was looking at her because he'd found syringes in the house, but they were medicine dispensers.

To the question had Brittany woken in the middle of the night, Ms. Hinson answered "no," saying both children sleep through the night and "never wake up." She also said there were no matches in the house and the only lighter was kept in her case and was childproof.

Ms. Hinson said that about 10:30, the night of the fire, she heard Josh cry so she took a flashlight so as not to wake the children, and went upstairs. Josh was asleep. So was Brittany. Ms. Hinson may have gone upstairs again at 12:00, because she "usually checks on them if she's awake, but she can't remember if she did that night.

SBI Interviews Firemen and Police Officers

On October 25, Special Agent White interviewed

volunteer fireman Tracy Fowler at his business address. Also present were Fire Chief Jerry Watts and Police Lt. Mike Glenn.

While Fowler was putting on his air pack, a police offer tells him, "The young-uns are upstairs. The girl is to my left and the boy is upstairs," but Fowler does not catch the rest of what the officer tells him.

As Fowler entered the residence and headed up the stairs, he was unable to get on his fire gloves because they were still wet from the previous fire that night.

At the top of the stairs, Fowler feels the heat, but sees no flames. He thinks he hears a little cry. While still trying to put on his fire gloves, he drops to his knees and begins walking on his knees toward the sound. His knees hit something. He finds a leg and then a head. The child is just inside the doorway, maybe four feet into the room, lying at an angle face down with her head toward the bed as if she were trying to get underneath the bed.

Fowler throws off his gloves, grabs the child under the chest and legs, walks out of the room on his knees to the landing, then stands to go downstairs. He cannot tell if the child is breathing. He does not hear her making any sounds.

After handing the child to a rescue worker, Fowler re-enters the residence and goes back upstairs, starts right, but stops when he sees Jeff Fowler coming out of that room (the mother's bedroom). He returns to the room to the left, thinking that both children could have been sleeping in the same room. Flames are now showing in the room straight ahead. He hears Jeff Fowler call, "I've got him!" Fowler turns around and sees Buddy Wally, a volunteer fireman, on a hose line on the landing.

Fowler's air bell is going off in his air pack. From behind, he grabs Jeff Fowler's straps to help him keep his balance as he goes down the stairs carrying the second child, as there are now hose lines going up the stairs.

Justice for Baby Josh

Outside, Jeff Fowler trips over the hose, falls, drops the child, who is picked up by a rescue worker and placed in a second ambulance.

Fowler concluded his interview with Special Agent White by saying that Columbus County 911 had been asked by the children's mother to have him call her on October 23. He did. The mother asked Fowler where he had found her daughter. He told her, "On the floor in her room."

The mother "started talking about the fire and all the damage that had been done and the room being completely destroyed." Fowler did not agree or disagree, but merely said "Uh-huh," indicating that he was listening. Finally, she said, "Thank you," but did not seem upset, nor was she crying when talking about the fire and her children. She sounded "nervous and was talking very fast."

October 25, SBI Interviews Jeffrey Fowler at his home. Also present is Tabor City Volunteer Fire Chief Jerry Watts.

Fowler tells SBI Agent White that firemen were pulling hose when he arrived by personal truck at 101 Wall St. Chief Watts was at the front door of the burning residence. Tracey Fowler was already inside the building looking for the children. A living room light is on.

Tracey Fowler comes down with the little girl. Jeff Fowler goes upstairs, turns left, finds no one, then goes into the room at the other end of the hall, again finding no child. He then starts into the last bedroom, where he observes no flames, but feels intense heat to his left as he crawls into the room. The smoke level is near the floor,

Fowler sees the leg of a crib, reaches in, grabs the baby, and leaves. As Jeff Fowler stands on the landing preparing to descend the stairs, Tracey Fowler grabs the straps holding Jeff 's air pack to help him down the stairs.

Once outside, Jeff Fowler trips on the fire hose, rolls on his side, spilling the baby on the ground. Ambulance driver Gary Watts picks up the baby, checks it's pulse, and places it in the back of the ambulance.

Fowler tells Agent White that he was having trouble with his face mask, was taking in smoke and had trouble breathing the whole time he was doing the search, which he estimates, took four to five minutes.

Fowler remembers seeing a heater on the upstairs landing and that it was located to the left of the little girl's room.

Russell reports seeing smoke coming from the top of the house, but no flames. He also did not see anyone standing at the door of the residence. As he got out of his car, Officer Moyer pulled in. As they both rush toward the house, the front door opens. A white female is standing in the doorway. Russell doesn't remember what she's wearing. She says, "get my kids. They're upstairs. One is to the left and one is straight ahead."

Russell follows Officer Moyer up the stairs. Four or five steps from the top, the two officers turn around because they can't breathe.

They then run to look for another way into the house. Finding none, they return to the front of the house where they find the woman talking on a cordless phone, in the living room, where she's been the entire time the two officers went around the house.

Russell reports that when he went back up the stairs, he did not feel any heat, but still could not breathe due to the smoke. The lights were off upstairs. Officer Russell sees a "little orange flame on the floor in front of him. He can no longer hold his breath and must go back downstairs.

Officers Russell and Moyer walk out of the house with the female as the firemen pull into the yard. One of the firemen is putting on turnout gear and a mask. Russell tells the fireman the children are upstairs but did not tell him which rooms they are in. Officer Russell then goes to block traffic at the corner of 6th and Wall Streets.

He recalls that the female told him she thought the electric radiator caused the fire upstairs and that was why she slept downstairs because of some problems with the downstairs radiator.

Russell did not notice any apparent burns or singed hair on the female, later identified as Terri Hinson.

October 25, SBI Agent White Interviews Corporal Gause

Officer Gause reports she was on her way home in her personal vehicle when she heard the fire call on her portable radio.
As she arrives, she sees Officer Moyer and Officer Russell walking out of the house with a woman holding a cordless

phone. The woman is wearing blue jeans, shoes, glasses, and a black silk jacket with an emblem on the back. As the fireman begin breaking out windows trying to get into the upstairs, Officer Gause and the woman move out of the yard to stand in the road.

Gause tells SBI Agent White she did not notice any burns on Hinson, who kept yelling, "Save my babies!" Gause says that due to the poor lighting, she could not tell if the woman's hair was singed. At that time, Hinson tells Gause that she has called her boyfriend to come pick her up. The woman also announces to Gause that her little boy is dead. (As yet, the children are still in the house.)

When the fireman brings out the little girl, Officer Gause tells Hinson, "Ma'am, there's your little girl" Hinson replies, "Where's my little boy?" The EMT places the little girl in the back of the ambulance, at which time Hinson says to Gause, "I can't lose it – I can't lose these. I've already lost two. If I lose these, they will have to kill me."

As Officer Gause heads over to the ambulance to check on the status of the little girl, Hinson starts walking toward the neighbor's house across the street, saying, "Get my children. Get my children out!" Trooper Lewis and his wife come out and take Hinson into their residence, but not before the fireman brings out the little boy. Hinson never asks to come over and look at her children or ask about her children. Hinson never makes any motion toward the ambulance where her little girl had been placed. Lt. Glenn of the Tabor City Police also goes inside the Lewis residence with Hinson.

The boyfriend arrives just as Hinson comes out of the Lewis home. Hinson gets in the car and leaves as the firemen are putting the fire out. "Hinson never asked what hospital the children were going to, or how her children were."

NEMAX Claims Service Report to USF&G Insurance

75

Origin and Cause Determination

This fire originated in the closet of the back bedroom. This opinion is supported by the burn patterns found on the structural members and the contents in this room as well as the statement of Terri Hinson, a resident and witness to this fire.

Based on the facts and circumstances presently known to me, this fire is being classified as having been caused by human hands. With the exception of the fire originating from some type of human involvement, all accidental ignition sources were considered and eliminated.

Fire Scene Evaluation

On Tuesday, October 22, 1996, 101 Wall Street, Tabor City, North Carolina was examined for the purposes of determining the origin and the cause of an October 20 fire. Present and providing access to the property were the tenants, Rodney Strickland and Terri Hinson, and one of the property owners, Michael Jones. Also present was Mr. Matt Mathews of USF&G Insurance.

The property at 101 Wall Street is a two-story, single family dwelling. It is a wood framed structure with brick veneer on the first floor and is approximately 26'x26'. It is over 30 years old. It is rented by Rodney Strickland, the primary tenant and his girlfriend, Terri Hinson. Ms. Hinson's two children, Brittany, age 4 and Joshua, age 17 months, lived there also. Joshua did not survive the fire. At the time of the fire, Mr. Strickland was away on a visitation with his son at the home of Mr. Strickland's mother in Fair Bluff, North Carolina.

I found the fire scene surrounded by yellow fire scene tape. Light ventilation stains were noted on each side of the house at the upstairs windows and gables. Some darkening of the upstairs windows was seen on the front of the dwelling. A hole in the roof was noted on the back to the left of a plumbing vent pipe. The upstairs windows on the back of the house were stained and broken out. An outside electric meter was located on the back of the house. The service conductors appear to run from the meter into the structure below the first floor. Telephone and cable TV service were noted on the Wall Street side. No gas service was noted. The fire pattern observed from the exterior indicated that the most fire damage was to the upstairs rear of the residence. There were no burn patterns on the first floor, although there was considerable water in the carpets. A utility room was located on the first floor at the back of the house where the 100 amp electrical service panel was found. Three 30-amp fuses were found to have been activated. There was no unusual electrical activity noted at the service panel. The electric water heater was located in the utility room and was noted to have been covered with clothing to dry. A portable electric heater was noted in the living room. It was plugged into an outlet under the window in the front of the house by way of a lightweight interior extension cord. The heater control switch was found in the "on" position. It was set at 1500 watts and the dial was at "9," the maximum setting. There was no electrical or fire damage noted to this heater, its power cord, the extension cord, or the outlet.

Upstairs, it was obvious that there had been previous alterations to this area by previous examinations. There were heat and smoke stains noted on the walls of the hallway upstairs. The smoke stains appeared to extend approximately 3 feet above the floor. There was a second portable heater located in the hallway. It was identical to the heater found in the living room. It was not plugged in. The power setting was at the lower wattage and the dial was at "9." There was no fire damage noted to this heater or its cord.

There are four rooms upstairs, three bedrooms and a bath. The entire upstairs was finished with painted tongue and groove pine planking on walls and ceilings. The master bedroom and Brittany's bedroom had heat and smoke damage. There was some fire extension noted in each, but it was limited to the doorways. A clock was found in the master bedroom. It had stopped at 3:56. The back bedroom (Josh's) had the heaviest fire damage. The door to this room had been removed presumably during previous examinations. It was found leaning against a wall in the hallway. The veneer portion of the door had been burned through at the top. The door and the jamb exhibited burn patterns that suggest this door had been partially open during the fire.

A closer examination of the fire patterns in this bedroom indicates that the fire originated in the closet on the bathroom side of the room. The closet doors appear to have been closed during the fire allowing the fire to progress until it broke through above them. It then appears to have progressed naturally throughout the room and eventually into the hallway and the other two bedrooms.

A duplex receptacle was found to the left of center on the back wall of the closet. It was examined and showed no signs of electrical activity or malfunctions. The burn patterns in the closet did not indicate that any heat had originated there. It appears that this receptacle was a victim of the fire. The burn patterns in the closet show more damage to the right side.

The attic area above the room of origin was examined. The roof above the closet had been burned through. A Romex conductor was found in the attic area that had run from the ceiling fixture in the room of origin to the fixture in the bathroom located behind the closet. The conductor showed no signs of electrical activity that would suggest it was the cause of this fire. The burn patterns in that area did not indicate that any heat had originated there. This conductor was a victim of the fire. The burn patterns found in the attic area indicate that the fire had burned up from the closet.

The physical evidence clearly shows the fire originating in the closet of the bedroom. This location sustained the greatest physical destruction and the tenant, Terri Hinson, reports the first observable flames emanating from there. There were no signs of an ignitable liquid having been present. The fixed wiring and electrical equipment in the area of origin showed no signs of arcing or failure. The tenant's list of contents in that closet does not contain any item(s) that would contribute to a fire cause. The same tenant reports having checked on the child sleeping in that room by flashlight at approximately 10:30 PM. The closet doors were closed and nothing unusual was noted. The tenant reports having smoked a cigarette for the first and only time in that room on Wednesday, three full days prior to the fire. She also stated that the last time she had been in that closet was on Friday.

With the elimination of available ignition sources, it must be concluded that this fire occurred due to some type of human action.

There were no smoke detectors found in the building. It is my understanding that rental property built before 1975 is not required to be protected by hard wired smoke detectors...

Investigation

A recorded statement was taken from the primary lease, Rodney Strickland, who stated he has been living at 101 Wall St. since May 1, 1996, is separated from his wife of 25 years, and lives there with Terri Hinson and her two children. At the time of the fire, he was at his mother's in Fair Bluff, NC, for a weekend visitation with his 14-year-old son. Terri Hinson called around 4:00 AM to tell him about the fire.

Terri Hinson told Strickland that night that she had noticed the power cord to the downstairs heater was warm to the touch. She slept downstairs so, in case something was to happen, she could be there. She was awakened and saw a red flicker at the stairwell. She tried to get the children but was unable to. Her hair was singed.

When he first moved in he had to replace three fuses, one Edison-based and two cartridge type. He has not had to replace any since. There were three light fixtures found hanging, two were in the kitchen and one in the living room. He put them back up and had no problem since. There have been no electrical problems since. They have been using power strips with surge protectors.

He did state that Terri thought that the lights had been dimming, but that he had not noticed it.

There were no smoke detectors in the house when he moved in. He had not purchased any.

There was a leak in the roof that started after Hurricane Fran. When it rained, water would leak through into the baby's room. There was enough water to wet the carpet. He remembers telling one of the owners about it.

Both he and Terri smoked in the house. He uses a childproof lighter and believes that she does also. He does not recall either of the children playing with a lighter or matches. He seldom has matches in the house.

October 22, A Recorded Statement of Terri Hinson
* The heater downstairs in the living room is warm to touch
* The children are put to bed around 7:00 PM
* She does school work and irons clothes while watching TV until 10:30 PM
* Joshua cries out in his sleep around 10:30 PM. She checks on him by flashlight. All OK.
* She falls asleep around 12:30 PM on the couch downstairs.
    * She is sleeping there in case the heater malfunctions. This heater is left on even though it was unusual to do so. The other heater is also left on even though it is identical to the one downstairs.

* She is awakened by Brittany calling, "Mommy, I'm
    scared." When she looks up, she sees a red-orange
    glow at top of the stairs,
* She runs up the stairs and sees flames coming out of
    Joshua's closet. She gets to his door when the fire
    comes out over her head. She hears Joshua call out
    twice.
* She calls for Brittany to come. She cannot see through the
    smoke.
* She runs downstairs to the kitchen and calls 911. She is
    talking to them when she goes back upstairs the
    second time. She hears Brittany calling again and tries
    to get her to come out. This time she cannot get past
    the top step. The police arrive and could not get any
    farther.
* She notes the heater downstairs is cold when she moves it.
* There are no lights on in the house. It is dark.
* The closet contains all of her clothing and Joshua's, also
    towels,
    wash cloths, sheets, and pillowcases, a tin popcorn
    container, a cardboard box, a plastic sewing box, and
    fish bowl.
* She had not been in that closet since Friday. The doors were
    usually
    closed. Brittany never went into the baby's room.
* The first and only time she smoked in that room was
    Wednesday while sorting out his clothing.
* Joshua was sick with a sinus infection at the time of the fire.

* She does not know how she managed to get hold of her
    shoes or glasses before ending up outside.
* She has three other children who were taken from her and
adopted.
* During the last week prior to the fire she noticed the lights
    in the kitchen and the living room would flicker.
* The leak in the roof was reported to Mr. Wright, a partner
    in ownership of the property with Mr. Jones. Someone
    showed up to look at the roof the week before the fire.
* She and Rodney discussed a possible move to another
apartment.

A phone call to Lt. Glenn on November 19, 1996.
    Glenn said that Corporal Brian Ramey of the Tabor
    City
 Police Department, prior tenant before Hinson, "distinctly
remembers purchasing four smoke detectors at Wal-Mart and
hanging them by double-sided tape throughout the house."
He left them there when he moved. Ramey also remembers
that the carpet in Joshua's room was very thick and that the
door was difficult to open and close.
    Lt. Glenn also related that Tabor City police officer
Robert Moyer had attempted to reach the children, but could
progress no further than the top of the stairs. According to
Moyer, a heavy smoke condition banking down to within 6-8
inches from the floor had driven him back, but not before
seeing an "orange glow at the top of the door, which appeared
to be closed. He also saw flames near the bottom of the door."

Comments
Because this fire involved a death, I recommended that the adjuster obtains another opinion as to the origin and cause. Accident Reconstruction of Raleigh, North Carolina was given the assignment on October 23, 1996. I have received a telephone report confirming my findings. Their report has not been received as of this writing.

November 19, 1996, SBI Reports Meeting with Brittany Hinson re: Cigarette Lighters

SBI Agents Matt White and T.K. West went to the residence of Bernice Simons Pierce, Terri's mother, with whom Brittany was presently living. Pierce and Brittany were exiting the front door of the residence onto the screened porch.

SA White spoke briefly with Pierce in reference to his showing Brittany some lighters to observe her reaction.

Pierce first telephoned Terri Hinson, then escorted SA West and SA White to the backyard, where Brittany had gone to play.

Pierce took one of the lighters from SA White and asked Brittany to look at the lighter that neither she nor the agents knew how to work.

Briefly, Brittany stopped and touched the lighter, holding it lightly in her right hand and then handed the lighter back to Pierce. Brittany stated that the lighter would burn her fingers and her hand, that it would hurt her, and she did not want to touch it.

Brittany showed no adverse emotion and played on a slide by SA West.

Pierce gave the lighter back to SA White.

Brittany came to SA West and hugged SA West's legs before SA West entered the SBI vehicle to leave.

The Arrest

On November 20, 1996, exactly 30 days after the fatal fire at 101 Wall Street, Tabor City, NC, Terri Hinson is stopped in the street by SBI Agent Matt White as her car approaches her mother's home at 1966 Main Street, Fair Bluff, North Carolina, where Terri Louise Hinson, DOB 4/24/64, is arrested for the First-Degree Murder of her infant son, Josh Cade Hinson, the First-Degree Attempted Murder of her four- year-old daughter Brittany Hinson, and for one count of First Degree Arson.

Back at the SBI office located in Whiteville, NC, Special Agent White advises Terri Hinson of her Miranda rights and then reads the waiver of rights. Hinson refuses to sign the waiver or to talk to White without a lawyer present.

Terri Hinson is placed in the Columbus County Jail in Whiteville, NC.

The following morning, Terri Hinson is arraigned on First Degree Murder, First Degree Attempted Murder, and First Degree Arson. The judge appoints Craig Wright as Hinson's attorney. Later, attorney Bill Wood joins Wright. Bail is denied pending the Grand Jury's findings.

Terri Hinson's first bond hearing is continued for a number of reasons, one of which had to do with her juvenile criminal history.

On January 15th, 1997, the second bond hearing results in bail being set at $200,000 and Terri Hinson being placed on "house arrest," with an ankle monitor. She and boyfriend Rodney Strickland move in with Terri Hinson's sister, Linda Hinson Smith. Terri requests visitation with Brittany.

January 6, 1997, SBI White Interviews Lorrie Lancaster, Tabor City Rescue Squad.

Also present are Rescue Squad members Gary Sikes,

and
Melissa Sykes, all who had been on the first ambulance which assisted in the rescue and transportation of Brittany Hinson the night of the fire.

Gary Sykes, the ambulance driver had just returned to the station from a prior call and was closing the bay door when he and his crew smelled smoke. As they remember, about 30 seconds later, they were paged to respond to a house fire on Wall Street.

As they pulled in behind the first fire truck, Lancaster observed Corporal Gause of the Tabor City Police and a white male officer at the scene. They also observed Defendant Terri Hinson with a cordless phone, wearing blue jeans, tennis shoes, and a short-sleeve shirt. Hinson came over to the ambulance and stated, "You made me leave my babies."

Gary Sikes asks where the children were located. Hinson pointed to a window in the front of the house facing Wall Street, which was actually the master bedroom.

Lancaster noted that Hinson's hair is singed, but only on its ends. She is not burned. Lancaster gives Hinson her jacket.

Hinson walked around the ambulance and started making several phone calls. Melissa Sykes overheard Hinson tell someone that her babies were burned. This was while the firemen were STILL trying to rescue the children. Hinson then walked down the road toward Trooper Lewis's driveway. Lancaster states that Hinson walked off by herself and was not asked to leave or taken away by the Tabor City patrol officers.

Lancaster stated Hinson was making phone calls before the first child was out of the building.

Gary Sykes tells SBI Agent White that he received Brittany from a fireman at the front door of the residence, that her body was limp, and that she was wearing one-piece footed pajamas, which showed no signs of burning. She smelled of smoke. Sykes says when he was at the door, the lights were still on but doesn't recall if they were still on when they left with Brittany for the hospital.

Lancaster stated she did not tell Hinson, who was some 20 yards down the road, that Brittany was out of the house. Lancaster stated the ambulance siren was not on, so Hinson would not have had to walk away from the ambulance to talk on the phone.

Lancaster stated she called on the radio for a second ambulance, which was operated by Ronnie and Sandra Watts, but once Joshua Hinson was placed in the second ambulance, it would be driven by volunteer fireman Gary Watts, who was formerly a Rescue Squad member. Lancaster's ambulance was leaving as the second ambulance arrived.

Hinson told Sykes and Lancaster, at the Loris Community Hospital that she was asleep on the couch when the fire started. They reported that Hinson had her glasses on and her cigarette case in her hand when she spoke to them.

In the ambulance on the way back from the hospital, Gary Sykes, Melissa Sykes, and Lorrie Lancaster all agreed that Hinson was "faking her emotions." Lancaster added that Hinson was not as upset as most people they had come in contact with, "even when they had fewer tragedies."

Melissa Sykes said that about two weeks later, she talked to Hinson about picking up some clothing for Brittany at the rescue center. At that time, Hinson denied setting the fire and couldn't understand why anyone would think she had. Hinson did not ask about the fire or where the children had been found.

January 6, 1997, SBI Agent White Interviews Gary Watts

Watts had been the volunteer fireman who drove the second ambulance carrying Joshua Hinson to the Loris

Hospital. Watts, a volunteer fireman, reported to the scene of the fire in his personal vehicle. He said he had "never laid eyes on Terri Hinson."

Gary Sykes told Watts that the baby was in the rear bedroom. There was already a double-staged ladder with a booster line at the back of the house. The window over the crib was broken out. The girl was already out of the house. Watts began spraying water into the room from below the window because of the "heat coming out of the window," drove Watts off the ladder as he only had his "turn-out coat" on.

Watts went around the house as Jeff Fowler was coming out of the house carrying the baby. Fowler tripped and fell to the ground. Watts picked up the baby and ran to the ambulance. He told Ronnie Watts, who had driven the ambulance to the fire, to get in the back and help with the baby. Gary Watts jumped into the front of the ambulance and drove to the Loris Hospital.

He denies ever talking with Hinson.

January 8, 1977, ACCIDENT RECONSTRUCTION REPORT

Personnel of Accident Reconstruction was asked to examine a house located in Tabor City, North Carolina that was damaged by fire on 8/25/96. (sic) (They've got the date wrong, which certainly makes one wonder about the accuracy of the rest of the report!) There was one fatality as a result of the fire. The structure was located at 101 Wall Street. The following report describes ARAI's investigation into the cause and origin of the fire.

The residential structure was a two-story house of wood construction with brick veneer and wood siding ...The large majority of the direct fire damage was confined to a second-floor bedroom and closet and adjacent attic space.

The double door closet showed the most severe fire damage, with floor level burn noted along the right side of the closet. The attic area and roof directly above the closet were also significantly damaged by the fire.

The remainder of the second floor, including the hallway, two additional bedrooms, and a bathroom, showed minor fire damage. The bedding and footboard of the northeast (master) bedroom on the second floor was burned, with the remainder of the room showing little fire damage. The cause of the burn to the bed, which appeared to be isolated from the rest of the fire, was not definitively determined. (Arsonists typically set fires in multiple locations.)

Based on the burn patterns, the origin of the fire was determined to be located in the closet of the northwest corner bedroom. The burn patterns showed that the fire started at floor level at the right side of the closet. Damage to the wood panel walls showed the fire burned upwards, eventually penetrating the ceiling and header above the closet doors. The header above the doors was burned from the inside outwards, and similarly, the closet ceiling joists were burned from the bottom to the top. The double swinging doors were at least partially open during the fire. The right closet door was burned more significantly than the left side door. The fire damage progressed from the closet into the bedroom in a typical "V" pattern. The remainder of the bedroom exhibited a lesser amount of fire damage as compared to the closet. It was noted that the bedroom door was closed during the fire, based on the burn patterns.

The contents of the closet were examined, and a description of the contents of the closet was obtained from the occupant of the house (through an interview with a previous fire investigator). There were no possible ignition sources determined from the contents of the closet.

There was an electrical outlet located on the back wall

of the closet on the left-hand side. There were no plugs in the outlet at the time of the fire. Inspection of the outlet and its associated wiring did not reveal any defects. The outlet was intact with the insulation remaining on the wires. The electrical outlet was not a possible ignition source of the fire.

A two-wire copper electrical conductor was noted in the attic over the left side of the closet. The insulation was consumed on the conductor in the area where the fire penetrated the roof of the closet and involved the overhead attic area. The insulation on the wire was intact in areas away from the damaged region. One of the conductors was separated, with melted copper visible on one of the wires away from the break. Examination of the break in the conductor showed fracture surfaces with mechanical damage as opposed to melting. The break was located mid-span between ceiling joists. The broken wire was traced and found to be the phase conductor for the two-wire set. The Conductor ran from the overhead fixture in the bedroom over the closet area and to the second-floor bathroom and was part of the circuit that serviced the second floor. The fuse for this circuit was blown (inside the fuse box.)

The conductor ran over the top of the ceiling joists, and the joist spaces were filled with insulation. Burn patterns to the ceiling joists near the conductor showed that they were burned from the bottom to the top, with the fire progressing from below the ceiling. In addition, close examination of the conductor showed that the phase and neutral wires contacted as a result of insulation damage caused by the fire. The conductor was not a possible ignition source for the fire.

The wiring in the attic area, the inside fuse panel, and the outside breaker panel were examined. There were no problems found with the electrical system of the house that would have caused the fire.

Conclusions

1. The fire originated inside the closet of the second-

floor bedroom in the northwest corner of the house. More specifically, the fire started on the floor at the right side of the closet.

2. There were no possible sources of ignition found with the structure's electrical system or the contents of the closet. The cause of the fire was undetermined.

The State of North Carolina v. Terri Louise Hinson

The State's case is, that in the absence of evidence that the fire which killed 17-month old Joshua Cade Hinson was caused by "accidental ignition sources," it must be "classified as a human hands fire." Only three people were present in the residence at the time of the fire, and who therefore had the opportunity to set the fire, namely the 17-month old victim, Josh Cade Hinson, who had been in his crib for nine hours before the fire, his four-year-old sister, Brittany Hinson, who herself was a victim, and who had demonstrated an aversion to cigarette lighters and on whom no ignition source had been found, and the Defendant, Terri Louise Hinson, who had both opportunity and means. (And multiple motives if the State had done its homework.)

The consensus of the arson and law enforcement investigators was that the fire originated in the closet of Joshua's bedroom next to the bathroom and that by means unknown and unspecified, Terri Hinson set the fire in that closet. No alternative place of origin was offered or suggested. Because the Defendant had testified that Brittany "never went in the baby's room, again leaving one to conclude that either 17-month-old Josh parachuted from his crib with some incendiary device – or his mother is the arsonist and murderer.

All electrical, mechanical, and "acts of God," had been examined and eliminated as causes of the fire. For example, the Defendant had made much of the space heater downstairs and its warm-to-the touch cord implying some kind of electrical malfunction had been the incendiary agent; however, an examination of the heater, its cord, and the outlet, found no evidence that these could have been a proximate or remote ignition source. (In truth, had investigators probed, they would have realized the Defendant was not tying the downstairs heater to the fire, so much as to justify her specious reason for having slept downstairs that night.)

The Defendant tried to blame Hurricane Fran, at one point exclaiming, "I know who killed my baby – Hurricane Fran!" And while the Hurricane had, in truth, occurred, the link between Fran and Josh's death was a stretch at best, and spurious at worst, the Defendant continued to hope fire investigators and law enforcement would join the Defendant in her inferential leap. None did.

The Defendant would have the State believe Hurricane Fran had caused water damage in the attic, which led the lights to flicker and dim, which in turn, resulted in an electrical fire in the attic, which just so happened to ignite over Josh's closet. Again, the NEMAX fire investigator examined the Romex electrical cable in the attic over Joshua's closet and found no evidence or arcing or other reasons to suspect an electrical cause of the fire. Accident Reconstruction of Raleigh confirmed NEMAX's conclusions.

Still, the State of North Carolina had put all their prosecutorial eggs in forensic logic's basket, and in so doing failed to look at the cornucopia of compelling circumstantial evidence, which could be used to strengthen their case in the event the Defense chose to wage a war of "hired-gun" experts. This was after all, the wires, conduits, and conductors had been shown to the jury, a case of a mother charged with murdering her infant son and attempting to murder her four-year-old daughter.

However compelling the forensic evidence might be, in order to win, the State would have to persuade a jury to believe the unbelievable, to wit, that in face of all we have experienced primordially about maternal instincts across most, if not all species, bout mother's dying to save their children, about mother's defending their young against any and all threats, this particular Defendant murdered her infant son. No woman, and few men, could conceptualize such cognitive dissonance!

The State of North Carolina failed to realize that no forensic evidence, short of a videotape of Terri Hinson setting the fire in Josh's closet, however compelling, could transform the surreal into a reality a jury would accept, and certainly not without even more compelling evidence to answer the question of motive.

But, the State of North Carolina, being solely represented by males, had no clue as to the societal upheaval this case would cause. Indeed, by charging a mother with murdering her child, to wit, Susan Smith, Diane Downs, and Dr. Greene, to whom she gave life, the State would be unwittingly attacking the very structure of the family, its assumptions, its reason for existence, hence the basis for the State itself, particularly the Ultra-Conservative Bible-Belt state of North Carolina, deluding itself of "holier-than-thou" and "family values" virtuosity.

Nevertheless, the State of North Carolina, being duly represented by male-dominated SBI, male-dominated law enforcement, and male dominated arson investigators and inspectors, oblivious to the need to make the unbelievable believable, ignored the "human side" – the emotional/psychological facet of the case, thereby setting themselves up for failure.

More specifically, the State failed to examine the Defendant's bizarre behavior, her contradictory statements, her implausible reasoning, and her obvious lying, with the same thoroughness they investigated the wires, heaters, and fuse boxes, with the result the State would be going to court without being able to present a plausible motive to the jury.

Without being able to answer the "why?" the State's forensic case was a sailboat without a sail. Without being told why Terri Hinson set fire to her son's bedroom, the jury would suspect they were being short-changed – that the States' case was incomplete, full of holes, not credible.

In the alternative, the Defense's case that she didn't do it would allow the jury to believe what they wanted to believe in the first place, to wit, that no mother is capable of murdering her own "flesh and blood."

For the Defense

In September, 1997, a year after the fire, the Defendant obtains a computer, sends her boyfriend scurrying for law books, and begins preparing for her trial.

In October, the Defendant uses the Internet to locate a Texas chemical engineer/arson expert, Dr. Hurst and begins receiving e-mail advice from Hurst regarding how to manage her case.

On October 31, 1997, the electrical fire investigator Wyman

Sox, hired by Terri Hinson's Attorney William Wood, and who therefore had a financial interest in proving his Defendant client's innocence, submits a report of his findings, in which Sox states, "These photographs indicated that the fire originated... in an area between the son's bedroom and the upstairs bathroom. The fire burned through the roof above the clothes closet... in the attic space above the clothes closet. Burn patterns to the ceiling joists and rafters show the concentration of fire in that area, burning through the roof."

Sox acknowledges, "The connecting Romex (cable) that was between the two listed lights in the son's bedroom and the bath ceiling was cut off and removed by others prior to my investigation," and that, "this wire was clearly cut by wire cutter-type pliers and removed leaving the remainder ends in the attic. This was a deliberate removal to destroy the evidence." Sox nevertheless had no qualms in concluding, "This fire was an accidental fire and the occupant (the Defendant whose Attorney had hired Sox) did not cause nor contribute to the damaged conductors."

On October 31, 1997, the Defendant's sister, Linda Hinson Smith writes the following letter to her sister's attorney, Craig Wright in which she claims she was the one, NOT her sister, who had gone behind her attorney's back and contacted self-described arson expert, Dr. Hurst.

> To: Craig Wright, Attorney
> From: Linda Hinson Smith
> Re: Terry Louise Hinson

Craig,

I wanted to share some information with you regarding the case you
are representing for my sister, Terri Louise Hinson.

Circumstances brought me back to Charlotte, however, the unfortunate situation Terri has been placed wrongfully in by the county of Columbus and State of North Carolina has remained a top priority for me. I have been doing my homework, so to speak and through doing so have come in contact with Mr. Gerald Hurst Chemist Consultant from Austin, Texas. It is my understanding Mr. Hurst has contacted you, offering his assistance on the case of Terri at no charge to you as her legal representative, her family and/or the State of North Carolina. Mr. Hurst has supplied you with his credentials which speak for their selves. I am sure you are in agreement that he could only be an asset to the defense for Terri. Since Mr. Hurst has offered his services free of charge, I would like to request you welcome his services and allow him to participate in the defense of Terri. In addition to his proven record in fire investigations, he also has professional relationships with others who would be of benefit to the case. I am very excited that a person of his stature, knowledgeability, credibility, and quality, in general, recognizes from the very limited information he has had access to the innocence of Terri and is offering to us his services, at no cost to top it off. Another prayer answered, I would say. I am sure you share this same excitement with me. My intentions are to speak with Terri, sharing with her my findings and this request to you to invite Mr. Hurst onto the case. I am sure she will be in total agreement. What reason do any of us have not to be?

I will ask Terri to call you regarding this. Thank you for your time, as always. Have a wonderful kind of day!

> cc: Mr. Gerald Hurst
> Terri Louise Hinson
> William Wood, Atty.

On November 10, 1997, Defendant Terri Hinson

sends the following note to her attorney, Craig Wright., again misleading him that it was her sister Linda who had initially contacted Hurst:

Mr. Wright,

I am writing this to let you know of the few things I have found missing from the discovery file. There are also some things I need for you to do. Please take a moment and look this over.

The files that are missing entirely:

The statement and/ or report from Chief Jerry Watts

The statement and /or report from Buddy Wallace (fireman on scene)

The statement and /or report from Ronnie and Sandra Watts

The statement and /or report from Godwin (fireman on scene)

The statement and /or report from Gary Sykes (ambulance)

The statement and /or report from Melissa Sykes (ambulance)

All of these should have written statements/reports

Pages missing from the reports we have:

Page 3 of Jeffrey Fowler (fireman)

Please see to it that we get a copy of these or if we cannot get a copy, that I am allowed to view them.

I would also like to view the pictures they took and the video. I need a copy of the 911 transcript or tape. I have noticed several discrepancies in the times everyone arrived. If I can get a record of what time each officer and fireman arrived, I can show definitive proof of who I told where Joshua and Brittany were (sic) located. I can show this now, but for real proof, I need the transcript so they cannot say they arrived at different times from what I have concluded from the given statements. I will be adding to this outline, I am sure. But this will give you an idea of what I am talking about.

As far as Mr. Hurst is concerned:

I understand from my sister that Dr. Gerald Hurst of Austin,

Texas has offered to review my case and get input from other fire investigation experts without any obligation on my part. I am enclosing an article from The Wall Street Journal describing one of Dr. Hurst's cases which bears a striking similarity to my own case.

Please send Dr. Hurst a copy of all the materials dealing with eye-witness reports, interviews, reports by fire, police and investigative agencies and photographs so that he can review them and possibly solicit advice from other experts willing to donate their time.

On February 5, 1998, the Defendant's sister, Linda Hinson Smith, sent the following letter to Judge Ola Bray, Columbus County Superior Court.

HONORABLE BRAY:

This letter is being written on behalf of Brittany Hinson, a niece currently at the mercy of Columbus County Social Services and State of North Carolina.

Brittany was removed from her mother's care due to a house fire in October, 1996 which at the time appeared to be of suspicious nature to local officials. She was taken from the Children's Hospital in Charleston, South Carolina after much-expressed concern of hospital officials that she needed to stay with family members due to her injuries and emotional well-being from the trauma of the fire, yet Social Services went against all recommendations and placed her in foster care. Per court order, she was later placed in the house of my mother, Bernice Prince. Brittany stayed with the grandmother until January 8, 1998. At this time my mother had a stroke and was hospitalized. All efforts were exhausted by the family to keep Brittany in familiar surroundings, including myself moving to my mother's home to care for Brittany and/or a requisition to have Brittany placed in my home. None of this was possible according to the Department of Social Services in Columbus County. This made absolutely no sense to me and still doesn't. I cannot comprehend why Social Services would rather see a child suffer emotionally by being completely uprooted from her family than to know the child is in a safe, loving environment with familiar people and surroundings. Not to mention the expense the county of Columbus and State of North Carolina is experiencing having to provide foster care. I am sure there are other children in that county which need and have no other alternative than foster care.

Justice for Baby Josh

Honorable Bray, I also understand her mother, Terri Hinson should have been given a minimum of two hearings from the point of Brittany's initial placement in my mother's home to prove to the State of North Carolina the allegations filed against her were not true and Brittany should not have been taken from her in the first place. She has had since December, 1996, proof without a doubt Brittany should be placed back with her yet our justice system has not given her the opportunity to do so. Our constitution states we are innocent until proven guilty. Does this apply everywhere except Columbus County? I am thoroughly frustrated with the manner in which Brittany has been handled. Marilyn Stevens, head of Guardian Ad Litem in Raleigh, North Carolina has expressed she does not understand herself why this has continued as long as it has, Brittany has been away from her mother too long and this should have been handled months ago. At the same time, local Guardian Ad Litem has not lived up to their part in this case. Home visits and studies have not been conducted, no one including Social Services has made an attempt to talk with Brittany to evaluate her emotional well-being and find just what is going on with this little girl. Everyone seems to be acting upon assumptions and you cannot <u>assume</u> being away from her mother is right in this case. Especially, when <u>facts</u> speak differently. Brittany is medically and mentally being neglected. Since being placed in foster care she has shown signs of medical needs and yet no one has acted upon this. If this is noticeable in a two-hour period on Tuesday and Thursdays by her mother and grandmother, the foster parent <u>has</u> to see it when Brittany is with her. Her school performance has declined, she is receiving spankings in school and I cannot help but believe this is due to the undue emotional stress she is experiencing thanks to the Department of Social Services, Columbus County.

Justice for Baby Josh

On or about January 16, 1998, I was informed paperwork has been forwarded to proper officials for placement in my home. Yesterday I receive a phone call from Aleisha Bowden, Department of Social Services, Columbus County informing my documents have not gone out but will be processed to go out today. Three more weeks wasted and all at a five-year-old's expense. Brittany's court appointed attorney has not done anything throughout this ordeal on her behalf, including the simple task of returning phone calls.

Honorable Bray, when we appeared before you in November 1996, you revealed to me to be a fair and caring person. As I sat in the Court Room observing your disposition in cases before you, careful and logical thought was given in each case. I am at wit's end. I see no reason for Brittany not to be placed in my home and God knows she will be very well taken care of and loved. The truth of the matter is, it is with her mother she needs to be. Until trial and/or dismissal, there is no justifiable reason for her to continue being away from her mother. There are two other adults in the home with Terri, one being the grandmother with a wonderful mind and the other Brittany's step-father. No guilt has been proven against Terri and will not be proven.

When a five-year-old cries the tears Brittany cries having to depart from her mother after her two-hour visitations on Tuesday and Thursdays wanting to stay with her mother, has to be "bribed" by the social worker to finally get Brittany to leave with her, stands in front of her school class and asks that everyone please pray for her and her mother to be together again soon, this is a child who needs to be with her mother. This is not a child abused by a mother. The only abuse, in this case, is child abuse by our system. One year, four months has passed in this child's life, time which can

100

never be given back to Brittany or her mother. The foundation of her little life is being cemented forever and there is not the first sensible thought process being used by the Department of Social Services or anyone who has played a part as an authoritative figure throughout this ordeal.

Honorable Bray, I have addressed this letter to you with the anticipated hope you can and will intervene. At this time, I nor my family can afford a private attorney for Brittany. At the same time, I nor my family can afford to see her little life being traumatized because of senseless actions of the Department of Social Services and State of North Carolina. I am sure if this were a child, niece, nephew of their family members they would have the same feelings and would do everything possible to turn the situation into a more favorable one for the child. As I mentioned to you earlier in this letter, the court appointed attorney has expressed no real concern in this case or any sense of urgency. If a child's well-being is not cause enough for a sense of urgency, then this world is in worse shape than I imagined.

Anything you can do to assist us in this matter will be greatly appreciated.

I await your reply.

With kindest regards,

Linda Hinson Smith

The Texas "Knight-Rider Arrives on His White Horse

On March 24, 1998, or 18 months after the fire, Dr. Hurst flies to North Carolina at his own expense to be an expert witness for the Defense. He is joined by an associate arson investigator Ken Gibson of Kemp Texas, and Wyman Sox of Columbia, SC, hired by the Defendant's lawyer. Hurst and Gibson stay several days.

On April 1, 1998, Hurst submits his findings to Columbus County District Attorney Lee Bollinger during a meeting in Bollinger's office. It is Hurst's opinion that:

1. The State of North Carolina erred in prosecuting Terri Hinson on the basis of a "negative corpus" argument, to wit, "eliminating all possible accidental and natural causes" and then concluding that the only person who could have started the fire (Terri Hinson), did, in fact, start the fire. Hurst maintains that "when the ignition source cannot, or was not, ascertained, the State is entitled to describe the cause of the fire as "undetermined," not "suspicious" or "arson". (According to Hurst's logic, the absence of physical evidence as to the cause of a fire does not prove person or persons guilty of arson. Is Hurst arguing "spontaneous combustion or "act of god?")? Well then, by the Hurst's rules of logic, he must neither claim nor imply that Terri Hinson is innocent of arson and murder. But, that is exactly what Hurst does AND gets by with it. Hurst uses the same bogus logic to declare Hinson's innocent that he used to rebut the State's evidence! Here is what he told DA Bollinger:

2. "Lacking physical evidence, the fire investigator," (which fire investigator? The SBI? The ATF Certified Fire Investigator? NEMAX? Accident Reconstruction of Raleigh? Fire Chief Jerry Watts, who all said Terri Hinson set the fire in Josh's bedroom, and they examined the fire scene 18 months BEFORE Hurst, and 18 months BEFORE the fire scene was contaminated by the wind, rain, and a parade of known and unknown persons removing, rearranging, and tampering with the fire scene evidence) "is strongly cautioned against" developing alternative hypotheses as to the fire's cause, i.e., to collect the insurance, hide other crimes, or

a pattern of pyromania. Wait a cotton pickin' minute! Hurst is wrongly equating motive with "cause." The State of North Carolina's case never confused "cause" with motive, nor did the State allege "to collect insurance, hide other crimes, nor a pattern of pyromania," either as "causes, or motives for the fire. In fact, it would be States' gross negligence in NOT establishing a motive, which would void their case against Terri Hinson.) "None of these secondary factors are present in this case and none of them would have been further developed in a well-run case...", i.e., Terri Hinson's "low economic status." Hurst reports, (again making illogical and unsubstantiated leaps and inferences more flagrant that those of which he accused the State of North Carolina) that, "The fact that Ms. Hinson had previously allowed the adoption of three children in a period of financial difficulty" (Your source, Dr. Hurst? Her own mother wrote to Social Services (Letter included in this book) charging Terri with abandoning her three children, by running off to Charlotte with her boyfriend, with whom she had been screwing while still married to the children's father!) "is proof enough that she would have been easily able to find her child (Joshua) a suitable home had she wished to free herself from responsibility." (Your source, Herr Doctor Hurst? My sources, namely her two former best friends and closest confidants, reported she tried to "dump" Josh on them, but turned her down when she would not promise timely visits with Josh. Your purported area of expertise is chemistry Dr. Hurst, NOT social work, in which your demonstrated ignorance is being used to deny Josh his day in court, and justice to the people of Columbus County and the State of North Carolina.)

3. "Because no incendiary "fire indicator" as listed in the National Fire Protection Association code 921 were found, none was used." (Wait a minute, Mr. Fire Expert! If the State of North Carolina can't use "negative corpus" to

convict, you can't use the "negative torchus" to acquit!)

4. Hurst argues there was also an absence of "potential factors not related to combustion, such as, remote location of the fire, fire near service equipment or appliances, removal or replacement of goods, absence of personal items, entry blocked or obstructed, sabotage to structure or fire protection, damage to fire-resistive assemblies, damage to fire protection systems, and open windows and exterior doors," without these "potential factors" present, there can be no arson. (Methinks, Dr. Hurst; you are presenting "junk science" to the DA Bollinger? For example, according to Tabor City patrolman Ramey, the previous tenant, bought and placed several smoke detectors up and downstairs, yet none were present at the time of the fire. If Ramey is telling the truth, and why wouldn't he, Terri and/or Rodney removed them, meeting the test of "potential factors of arson" #8 --"damage to fire protection systems."

The only other entrance to the house was a side door, which Officers Russell and Moyer tried to enter, but could not because the door was locked and blocked by a table, thereby meeting #5 "entry blocked or obstructed" in your test of "potential factors for arson."

"Remote location of the fire," test #1: The consensus is that the fire started in the far back corner of Josh's upstairs bedroom closet, the most remote place in the house.

"Fire near service equipment or appliances," test# 2: the outlet in Josh's closet was used by Terri to do her ironing and run Josh's vaporizer.

"Removal or replacement of goods, test #3: hours after the fire, officer Gause saw Strickland and Hinson crossing the taped crime scene removing objects from the burned house into their car. They returned that afternoon and again on Monday to remove more "goods".

"Absence of personal items," test #4: Police, Rescue Squad, firemen, and neighbors unanimously reported seeing

Terri Hinson fully dressed at 4:00 AM on Sunday morning, wearing glasses, carrying a cigarette case in one hand and her phone in the other, dressed and ready to remove her most personal item herself from the house as soon as Mission Accomplished.

"Sabotage to the structure or fire protection," test #6: the evidence suggests that Terri Hinson, at various times, "sabotaged" Josh's closet and bedroom doors to both maximize the fire and then close his bedroom door to make certain he died in the fire.

"Open windows and doors, test #9: "Hinson reports seeing the lights from the arriving police cars from inside the house and then stating the downstairs heater was "cool," when she moved it out of the way so the policemen could get up the stairs. How would this heater, the sole source of heat for the downstairs, where "cold-natured" Hinson claimed to be sleeping, in a T-shirt, be "cold to the touch?" The fire set, what better way to fan the flames, than to open the front door, sucking the cold night air up the stairs, through Josh's bedroom door, into the closet and out through the roof in his closet in a ball of fire, after first cooling the heater at the front door? Hinson closed the front door, after closing Josh's door and just before calling 911.

All Hurst's requirements of "potential factors" for a finding of arson having been met, it would seem that Dr. Hurst, having been conned by Hinson as to her innocence before he left Texas, and an ego bigger than his brain, he had to choose but to cook the books, to convince DA Bollinger that his "junk science" was spoken *ex-cathedra.*

5. "The fire scene showed only two significant areas of burning," Joshua's closet and the attic area above his closet, with the "heaviest burning in the attic where sections of rafters and joists were completely consumed immediately above the closet. These wooden beams were the most massive specimens destroyed in the fire and therefore, undisputedly

identify the area of deepest penetration and charring." (Or, because the beams acted as grates for the flames roaring up through the roof from the floor below. Because a charcoal grill gets hot to cook, does not mean the fire itself does not emanate from the coals below. Apparently, Texas is the only place on Planet Earth where fire burns down. Hurst would have Bollinger believe the damage in the closet was caused by fall-down from the attic onto the floor of the closet, meaning "massive" ceiling joists crashed to the floor without waking either Josh, Brittany, or their mother, who claims she was awakened by Brittany's voice saying, "I'm scared." More junk science!)

    6. "SBI Agent Matt White and ATF Special Agent Frank Malter investigated the fire scene and concluded erroneously, that because the underside of the closet shelf was more heavily burned than the top, the fire must have originated on the floor, or at least, beneath the shelf." (a year and a half after wind and rain damage and possible evidence tampering, Hurst opines the inflamed joists noiselessly fell to the floor, somehow negotiated their fall so as to avoid hitting the closet shelves, then miraculously started burning under the same shelf. No wonder Hurst's services were free.)

    7. "SBI Agent Matt White and ATF Agent Malter found no signs of electrical overheating at the outlet, and therefore determined, in error, that the fire was not caused by faulty wiring. In so doing, they ignored the attic Romex cable "bent down into the closet hole" with three independent areas of damage which "could constitute signatures of an electrical origin." ("Could!" "Might have!" "Maybe!" "Possibly!" – but definitely NOT according to two independent fire investigations, namely NEMAX, who examined "a Romex conductor" two days after the fire, and concluded, "This conductor showed no signs of electrical activity that would suggest it was the cause of this fire." Similarly, in their report, Accident Reconstruction Analysis, Inc., concluded, "The

(Romex) conductor was not a possible ignition source for the fire." (So why did Hurst fail to mention either the NEMAX or Accident Reconstruction Analysis findings to Bollinger? Because, he left Texas conned into believing Hinson was innocent and had neither the courage nor the integrity to admit he'd been "took," by Hinson.)

(Why did Hurst fail to admit to Bollinger that the Romex cable had been cut long before Hurst arrived, thereby severely contaminating his findings? Same reason.)

(a) The break in the wire, if occurring before the fire, could ("could"? is not "did") have yielded "up to approximately 25 watts of local energy release."

(b) The "electrical arc" damage, could ("could" sounds desperate) have caused the fire, but cannot be proven to have occurred before, during, (or after), the fire.

(c) The melted wire could ("could")have been caused by "electrical phenomenon" leading to possible ("possible") ignition, but the melted conductor destroyed "any evidence of a causative arc."

8. The SBI and ATF investigators failed to consider the effects of the "sudden drop in temperature" on increased electrical load and possible condensation "leading to increased propensity to arc tracking." (Yes, but if you'd done your homework, Dr. Hurst you would have seen that both NEMAX and Accident Reconstruction eliminated electrical loading as contributors to the fire. But then, you would have to admit you'd been conned and had flown to North Carolina for a week to rescue an arsonist and murderer.)

9. The heavier burning in the closet under the shelf does not prove the fire started beneath the shelf," because the objects on top of the shelf, i.e., folded bedding, towels, and box of glasses, would have been "insulating properties" of these materials and "the inevitable effects of fall down on the particular fuel load under the shelf." "Below the shelf, there were hanging clothes, which because of their loose vertical

orientation, act as accelerants, burning rapidly as long as oxygen is available. Any fall down from the ceiling or roof would ignite the hanging clothes and produce an intense fire under the shelf. The heavier, rapid burning would occur under the portion of shelving that was immediately above the garments and to the wall which was closest to them." (So, "Doc" maybe these clothes WERE the accelerants! Terri Hinson's cigarette lighter applied to the bottom of hanging clothing known to be inflammable would be a convenient torch, n'est pas?)

10. The contrast between the attic and room fire damage "shows the fire burned long before creating an open path to the room", i.e., "the damage is progressively less going from the attic to the closet to the bedroom," therefore, because investigators could not agree on whether the closet doors were open or shut, "at the very least," the fire patterns suggest the fire started in the attic." (Gee, Dr. Hurst, you missed your calling. Anyone who can twist the truth with such facility would have made a fortune as a defense attorney.)

11. "The circular burn pattern in Joshua's closet floor was seen by the SBI as indicating the door was open as determined by investigators the day after the fire. However, it is more likely that the burn floor pattern was caused by fallen material "dropping in flames" from the attic. (And snow falls up, that's why the top of the mountain gets more snow than the valley.)

12. Frank Magini, NEMAX investigator for USF&G, the insurer of the property, concurred with SBI and ATF investigators that the fire had been caused by "some type of human action," and that the Romex cable "showed no signs of electrical activity that would suggest it was the cause of the fire, "without noting that one conductor was broken and without looking at the wire closely. (Wrong! Both NEMAX and Accident Reconstruction examined the Romex cable

"closely" and did so two days after the fire, not 18 months later, as you did Mr. Hurst, and not after the cable had been cut and a section removed!)

13. "Five days after the fire, USF&G mechanical engineer Michael Sutton, found that the closet door had been closed at the time of the fire and that the ceiling joists had burned "from the bottom to the top. Nevertheless, Hurst argues, "But fire patterns may simply show the last direction of the fire, not the first. ("May simply!" Is this a fire investigation report or a "laying on of glands"?)

14. "The fact is that there is no accepted method of proving that an arc was the result of a fire"... and to determine if "an arc starts a fire can sometimes be shown by microscopic examination of the grain structure of the portion of the wire adjacent to the bead ..." (But Hurst said earlier that, "This wire ... had three independent areas of damage which could constitute signatures of an electrical origin.")

15. "I will not comment on the materials apparently gathered in the unsuccessful search for some motive for a mother to murder her youngest child." (Good! Don't. You're a chemist, not a shrink.)   16. In a small town like Tabor City, there is likely to be "conflicts of interest among witnesses" leading "to errors in communication" among police, fire, and rescue personnel which could have "unintentionally hindered the rescue of Joshua Cade before he died of carbon monoxide poisoning." (Damn! You just did what you promised you wouldn't do! Worse, after less than a week among the good folks of Tabor City, you now blame them for Josh's death! I don't know about Texas folks, but after 20 plus years here in North Carolina, I'd expect a cross-burning on my lawn or a drive-by shooting for accusing folks, especially those who risked their lives to save Brittany and Josh, of being a hindrance to saving Josh's life. I just hope you made your plane reservation in advance. Besides, Dr.

Hurst before you impugn the motives of the folks in Tabor City, how about coming clean regarding your own "conflict of interest." Didn't you fly from Texas to North Carolina at your own expense in order to free a damsel in distress, and thus get your name on the national news? You could only do that by persuading the Columbus County District Attorney that Terri Hinson did not start the fire which resulted in her son's death and her daughter's near death. Your mission was to get her case dismissed to enhance your reputation, so that the fee you could then charge other folks who could afford you would double -- truth and justice for baby Josh be damned!)

Not surprisingly, Hurst concluded his report by stating, "Clearly there is no physical evidence in the Terri Hinson case that will support the conclusions of the prosecution experts with respect to an incendiary origin of the fire." (Fraud, liar, snake oil salesman, charlatan, or all of the above?)

Infants Don't Vote

On April 16, 1998, Columbus County Assistant District Attorney, Lee Bollinger, dismissed the charges of First Degree Murder, Attempted First Degree Murder, and First Degree Arson against Defendant Terri L. Hinson, reasoning, "Review of cause and origin evidence from additional experts (Dr. Hurst) who were not available to the State prior to indictments being returned by the Grand Jury in this case."

(Hold on! Bollinger! Hurst's Report was a fraud. A sham! Hurst's testimony was based on "could's and "maybes" -- speculation grounded on a contaminated crime scene 18 months after the fire! How can you justify ruling for Hurst and against the ATF Certified investigator's report, the NEMAX findings, the Accident Reconstruction Report, your own SBI, and the only fire expert who was actually at the fire, Tabor City Fire Chief Jerry Watts?

If you weren't satisfied with the State's investigation in general, and the lack of evidence for Hinson's motive, you had 18 months to instruct law enforcement to find the motive. You now compound your dereliction of duty by letting Terri Hinson get away with murder because you failed to do your job!

Are you one of those Conservative right-to-lifer male politicians who foam at the mouth, so exorcised that you call abortion of a pre-human "murder," while, the hypocrisy of hypocrisies - you let a mother go free, despite the preponderance of physical and circumstantial evidence that she torched her baby?

By what right do you presume to be judge and jury, when your job is supposed to be limited to prosecutor? Isn't it the law of the land that a jury, not you, should decide to believe Hurst or NEMAX, the ATF, Accident Reconstruction, and the SBI?

Who was representing Josh? Oh, I forgot, infants don't have
lobbyists, don't belong to PACS, can't make campaign contributions, or even vote, especially dead infants.

But this is the South – Apartheid American style – plantation owner/slave culture, in which no one questions "the Man".)

On Tuesday, April 21, 1998, the Fayetteville, North Carolina, *Observer-Times*, ran the following spin.

"Internet Helps Clear Columbus County Woman"

Whiteville - Terri Hinson Strickland says she never doubted that arson and murder charges filed against her in the 1996 death of her 17-month-old son would be proved false.

But she never expected to use her home computer to find experts to argue her case.

Joshua Hinson died in an Oct. 20, 1996, blaze at his mother's 101 Wall St. home in Tabor City. Firefighters responding to the early morning call found Joshua dead in his crib, and his sister Brittany, then 4, on the floor of her room. Brittany recovered from her injuries.

All charges against Strickland, now 34 and living with her mother in Fair Bluff, were dismissed by Assistant District Attorney Lee Bollinger Friday. Bollinger says he made his decision after an April 1 meeting with three arson experts Strickland found through the Internet.

"After listening to them, talking again to our fire scene investigators, it was our determination that we could not determine that she set the fire," Bollinger said. ("our" meaning the DA, getting re-elected.)

Bollinger opined "there was strong, but not conclusive evidence, that the fire began in 50-year old wiring above a closet in Joshua's upstairs room in the two-story home." (Bollinger had sold his political soul to the devil, whoops, I mean his boss, the Columbus County District Attorney).

"That particular Romex cable is what we cannot eliminate as a potential cause of the fire," Bollinger said. "When you look at it in close detail, all the physical evidence there at the scene, you really can't say beyond a reasonable doubt that she set the fire, or that the wire was responsible. ("Reasonable doubt" is for the jury to determine, not the elected Columbus County District Attorney). "What you can say is that the cause of this fire is undetermined and that all the experts have nothing more than subjective opinions on how the fire started."

"The more we did, the more we realized that the case boiled down to cause and origin of the fire," he said. "We have absolutely no case of motive or other circumstances that would tend to show how it started." (Oh, how wrong you are

Mr. Bollinger and what a gross injustice you and your boss have perpetrated against a murdered infant and the citizens of Columbus County!)

Bollinger said the State had "an ethical obligation to dismiss" the charges against Strickland. (No, as the lead prosecutor in Columbus County, Bollinger had an ethical obligation to a dead Baby Josh Hinson to assure him his day in court. Instead, it appears Bollinger, like the God of Abraham, sacrificed baby Josh on the altar of his shameless political self- interests, to wit, making certain he and his boss didn't offend woman voters in Columbus County.)

Bollinger said his only regret was that the State did not have the resources to get experts with the credentials of those who supported Strickland. (Bollinger had the "experts" at ATF, the SBI, NEMAX, Accident Reconstruction, and Fire Chief Watts. He ignored their "expert" testimony because it risked his boss's re-election plans.)

"The men who met with Bollinger April 1 came to North Carolina at their own expense and refused compensation, Bollinger said. (Bad logic by Bollinger: Their coming to North Carolina biased and invalidated their testimony. They'd made up their minds Hinson was innocent, before they left Texas, making their investigation a fraud. Therefore, Bollinger's presumption that because they refused compensation, their investigation deserves credibility, on its face, lacks credibility. Third, what Hurst lost in plane fare, he schemed to recoup four-fold in his marketable reputation.)

"The arson experts who met Bollinger included Dr. Gerald Hurst of Texas, a Cambridge-educated chemist; Ken Gibson, an expert in fire investigations with some 30 years of experience in Texas, and Wyman Sox, a fire investigator from Raleigh hired by Strickland's lawyers, Craig Wright and Bill Woods. (And for the State, Bollinger had the Certified ATF investigator, the SBI, NEMAX Fire investigators, Accident Reconstruction of Raleigh, and the only one of the bunch who was actually at the fire, Chief Watts, who probably had more fire investigative experience in the trenches, than any of the Texas crew.

Strickland says it was Hurst and Gibson who made a real difference, as well as an Australian arson expert named Tony Caf, who she also found on the Internet. (Who? When did Caf ever investigate the crime scene?)

"The Internet was my starting point," she said. "Tony was willing to come here too, but he wasn't sure if they would accept his credentials from Australia. When they saw the evidence, they believed me. (No, you had convinced them of your version of what happened on the night of October 20, 1996, before they bought their round-trip plane tickets.) "These gentlemen know their jobs. I owe them my life, I really do." (Indeed, you do. Without their flawed, fraud, and tainted testimony to Bollinger, your life could have ended in an electric chair in Central Prison, and you certainly would not have gotten by with a perfect murder. But your real debt of gratitude is owed Mr. Bollinger, and his boss, the District Attorney of Columbus County. By choosing to trump prosecuting you with the DA's own political ambitions, he alone saved you from execution or a life sentence at Woman's Prison.)

"Strickland, who married her long-time boyfriend, Rodney Strickland last May 23, said her first priority now is to get her daughter Brittany back, and then get on with her life."

"Brittany was taken from her mother after the arrest and has been living with family members, most recently a sister in Charlotte. A hearing today was expected to result in the return of Brittany to her mother's custody."

"As soon as the hearing is over, I'm going to Charlotte to get my little girl," Strickland said. "We'll go on; we'll have our lives. We're very close." (So close, you didn't even ride with Brittany in the ambulance, while the Tabor

City Rescue Squad worked and prayed to keep Brittany alive!) "She's suffered, but she's pretty resilient." (Brittany better be more than resilient, if she ever finds out what really happened on the night of October 20, 1996.)

"I think to do what I've had to do, to go through the last 18 months and still have my sanity, I have to have something in there." (Yes, indeed. That something is called, by those more disposed to be more charitable than this writer, "larceny in one's soul.")

"But Josh is not here ... my son is gone and no amount of anything can bring him back. My son should not have died, and that's something I have to deal with." (You might write to Susan Smith, Diane Downs, Dr. Greene, *et al*, saying, "See, that's how a mom commits the perfect murder.")

"Before the fire, and before her arrest, Strickland was completing studies toward an Associate's Degree in criminal justice from Southeastern Community College. She will not go back."

"That was not right, it was not fair what happened to me. It's made me have a whole different outlook on criminal justice." (Besides, I got what I needed to commit a perfect murder.)

How the State of North Carolina, the SBI, and the District Attorney of Columbus County Committed Baby Josh to a Second Death, as Cruel and Unjust as the First

Perhaps the Columbus County District Attorney can be pitied for having too willingly capitulated to Dr. Hurst's biased, flawed, and speculative conclusions, so as not to offend the women voters of Columbus County. After all, putting a mom on trial for the murder of her infant son, *ipso facto*, might suggest that the DA is a male chauvinist anti-women bully. More certainly, should he fail to convict Hinson, sufficient female voters would have their suspicions confirmed to put his re-election and his political future at risk.

Even suggesting a mother in Columbus County could commit such a heinous crime, would betray the delusion that the good and decent folks in Columbus County are incapable of such a horrific act.

So, sacrificing an infant from the wrong side of the tracks (Didn't one of the Hinson boys die in a shootout with the Sheriff on Main Street back in the 40's in a dispute over taxi fares?) in order to protect his political future was a no-brainer for the DA. Besides, Josh's father had disowned him and his mother had already put three of her children out for adoption, so hey, even if she hadn't actually torched his bedroom while he slept, she also hadn't done what most mothers would have done to save him. So, why should the DA risk his re-election on a kid no one wanted. He shouldn't He didn't.

Hurst's report delivered the DA an "out". All he had to do was put the right spin in the newspapers, to wit, that in the battle of the experts, Hinson's experts won. Don't even mention the reports from ATF, NEMAX, Accident Reconstruction, throw his own SBI investigators under the bus, and hide behind the "Doctor" tag on Hurst's calling card. Make the Hinson story as a happy ending with mother and surviving child being reunited and Hinson and her adulterous live-in boyfriend getting married.

Tell the reader what they want to believe, not the ugly truth that the Columbus County District Attorney had aided and abetted a mom's perfect murder of her infant son.

As H.L. Mencken observed, "The men the American people admire most extravagantly are the most daring liars; (Billy Graham and Ronald Reagan) the men they detest most violently are those who try to tell them the truth." (Thomas Paine and Howard Zinn).

The Columbus County District Attorney, depending on the electorate's vote, wanted no part in either telling or ascertaining, the truth as to the matters related to the events of October 20, 1996. The public's right to know-- the DA's job to prosecute the offender, and acting honorably and ethically be damned!

Mom's Motives Missed by Both Sides

Dr. Hurst, *et al*, failed to discern the mom's motives because, (1) Hurst was a chemical engineer, and as such unqualified to investigate motives, even though being unqualified did not give him pause before pontificating that Terri Hinson was the victim of "conflicts of interest among witnesses." (2) Hurst hadn't flown in from Texas at his own expense to look for Hinson's motives. and (3) Hurst could only, 18 months AFTER the fire, be governed by his own self-interests to look for physical evidence, and/or contrive theories to acquit Hinson. He needed no motive because he had been duped into believing she was innocent before he set foot in the airport in Texas.

Ok, so what's the SBI's excuse? In retrospect, it would seem the Columbus County DA blind-sided Agent Matt White Agent T. K. West – threw them under the bus to preserve the DA's future electability.

Justice for Baby Josh

Until Bollinger dismissed all charges against Terri Hinson, on April 16, 1998, the SBI had every reason to believe their case against Terri Louise Hinson to be a "slam dunk" – all natural, electrical, mechanical, and "act of god" causes of the fire having been eliminated, meaning the fire was done by "human hands," and with only six hands being present and having the opportunity, and with four of the six ruled out, only the mother's hands were left. The fact that the mother had three "priors," to wit, documents showed she had signed adoption papers on three of her prior children, the SBI arrested and charged the mother, Terri Hinson with First Degree Murder, First Degree Attempted Murder, and First Degree Arson, on November 30, 1996, 30 days after the fire, confident they would successfully convict Hinson – so confident that male agents White and West failed to look for a motive – ironies of ironies – a fatal mistake women investigators would never have made,

And from all appearances, the District Attorney in Columbus County, and whoever else was responsible for directing the investigation, failed to instruct the SBI agents to answer the question: What was Hinson's motive for torching her children?

Of course, Hinson claimed to the investigators to have loved her infant son Josh. But how does her claim fit the fact that instead of riding with her dead or dying son in the ambulance, she chose, according to all the witnesses at the fire, to wait for her boyfriend?

Mom's motives? According to Josh's grandmother, Josh's father had been duped by Terri Hinson into believing she couldn't bear any more children. (Sound familiar? She'd previously duped Brittany's father.) She'd reported that a kidney operation had rendered her infertile, or so she reportedly volunteered to Josh's father and Josh's paternal grandparents, who were no less unhappy about having Terry Hinson hanging around their son.

Justice for Baby Josh

Was Hinson offering their son "safe sex" under false pretenses, as part of her scheme to get pregnant, thereby forcing her future in-laws to relent to give this "southern white-trash" passage into the Big House?

Safe sex, indeed! She became pregnant according to plan, except Josh's father, taking exception to being duped by Hinson, fled to parts unknown, telling Hinson he didn't even want his name on the birth certificate.

Her plan failed, she was left with a child she wanted only as a means to an end, namely, as a way to escape from the "southern white trash" class into which she had been born and had lived in up until now, into membership into the class of upper- middle-class home, she would never otherwise achieve.

But being unwilling to stop smoking during her pregnancy, Hinson gave birth to a low, birth-weight, sickly child, needing to be on a apnea monitor, a child whose bad health required his mother to keep him with her at all times, a child destined to have serious learning disabilities if he lived long enough, and a child requiring more mothering from a mother with a history of providing less – much less – a history of parental negligence, child abuse, and abandonment.

What had Terri Hinson done in the past when she had to choose between a boyfriend and her children? Abandonment and adoption, that's what. But who would take Josh, an unwanted, unneeded, runny-nosed, sickly, and developmentally-issued child?

Lord knows Terri tried. She begged her two closest friends, at various times to "take" Josh, meaning informally adopt him – "keep him. I don't want him." In fact, she allegedly asked her friend Betty Gore to "take" Josh less than two weeks before the fire.

Sounds like a desperate motive for arson and murder to me. How about you?

Motive #2. And there are those who allegedly

119

overheard her boyfriend Rodney Strickland state on a number of occasions, "I've already raised two young-uns of my own, I ain't planning raisin' someone else's," meaning Josh and Brittany.

A similar remark by Susan Smith's boyfriend landed her son's Alex and Michael strapped into their seat belts at the bottom of John D. Long Lake, in Union South Carolina, n'est pas?

Motive #3. Friends reported that Terri put both Brittany and Josh to bed at 7:00 PM, "to get them out of her way." There are also reports of Terri constantly demanding that friends and her mother "come and get the kids, so I can do what I need to do." From her history, Terri has used sex and having children as a way of controlling the man in her life at the time. There is no evidence she wanted children for their own sake, and that as soon as she had to choose between her own enjoyment and their well-being and care, she chose the former and neglected the latter.

Josh, being an especially needy child, promised Terri a life of caring for her son at a level she was neither capable of providing, even if she wanted to, which she certainly did not.

Her friends refused to take him and she'd already put up three earlier children for adoption, meaning she'd gone to the adoption well too many times. The only solution was to torch Josh's bedroom, a scheme made more palatable given her inability to bond with anyone, including her children.

Motive #4. Being unable to bond, Terri's children became expendable. Being unable to bond, she substituted control for bonding in all her relationships. (This issue will soon receive a more 'clinical" exegesis in the following pages.) In the meantime, we must consider her relationship with her current boyfriend Rodney Strickland at the time of the fire on October 20, 1996, who like all her others, was picked as being someone she could control. Hadn't she lured him away from his wife and sons with sex? Hadn't she waged an unwarranted, unrelenting, desperate propaganda/slanderous war against Rodney's wife and his two sons? Hasn't she done everything she could to alienate Rodney from his former family? Hadn't she drafted Rodney's Separation Agreement? And hadn't she threatened Rodney that something, "Bad will happen if you leave me to go to Fair Bluff this weekend for visitation."? (The Saturday before the fire early Sunday morning.)

In Terri's desperate world to absolutely control Rodney, his trip to his ex-wife's, that Saturday night before the Sunday fire, threatened to destroy everything Terri had done to win control of Rodney away from his wife and sons. In her view, he was just likely to stay up in Fair Bluff with his wife as return to Tabor City.

Something had to be done. It was, and it was the "baddest of bad" -- Terri set fire to her house, killed Josh, and nearly killed Brittany, giving a modern twist to *Medea*, the play by Euripides.

Motive #5. Rodney was expecting a lump sum Workman's Comp settlement of some $20,000, a fortune to Terri Hinson who had been milking Welfare, Food Stamps, and Pell grants for years. She would see none of the settlement unless she could get Rodney to marry her, and he said he wasn't going to be "raisin' someone else's kids," meaning Terri's Brittany and Josh.

Motive #6. The house Rodney had rented and in which Terri and her two children were living was old – over 50 years old. The electrical system seemed original. Sometimes the lights flickered, Hurricane Fran hit on September 5th, shearing off shingles and alleging causing Josh's ceiling to leak.

The house was jointly owned by a Mr. Mike Jones who owned several stores in the area and Tabor City Attorney Richard Wright. Terri smelled money – lots of money; she wanted some sum, but how? The solution? A fire made to look as if it had been caused by old wiring. Josh, for sure, and Brittany maybe, die in the fire, Terri gets out in time because she's sleeping fully dressed downstairs near the only working door, and Bingo! She collects a bundle by prevailing in a wrongful death suit. (Friends visiting Terri at her mother's house that Sunday afternoon, some eight hours after the Sunday 4:00 AM fire, reported being dismayed that Terri had yet to go to Charleston, SC Burn Center where Brittany was fighting for her life, and that rather than grieving over Josh's death, Terri and her family were scheming how best to sue her two landlords.)

Beyond the State of North Carolina's failure to establish motives for Terri Hinson's alleged arson and murder, by focusing on electrical outlets, wires, and Romex cables, the State failed to develop the preponderance of circumstantial evidence lurking behind each and every of the multiple contradictory statements made by Hinson in describing the events and her behavior on the early morning of October 20, 1996.

For example, both police officers first to the scene reported seeing orange flames behind the door at the head of the stairs as they tried to go up the stairs to rescue Josh and his sister. Why would Josh's door be closed when his mother told investigators she had placed a heater outside the children's door on that first chilly October night to warm Josh's and Brittany's bedrooms? The only reason for his door to be shut would have been to make sure he died in the fire.

And this is only one of many disparities the SBI failed to examine. Indeed, the State of North Carolina failed to interview Terri Hinson's ex-husbands, ex-boyfriends, the many fathers of her five children, her two closest friends, her closest friend's boyfriend – himself a fireman who had answered Terri's question about "Fire-over" – that "whoosh" she reported coming at from Josh's room. The State of North

Carolina also failed to interview Terri's hairdresser/confessor, or, on point as to motive, Josh's paternal grandmother, who, as just noted above, would allege Terri Hinson's scheme to use her fraudulent pregnancy with Josh to finagle her way into "The Big House." What of motives for murder accruing from Strickland's Workman's Comp case, which Josh's existence threatened, and Terri Hinson's plan to sue her wealthy landlords for the wrongful death of her two children?

Terri Hinson had told SBI investigator Matt White that her three previous children had been "taken" from her and placed for adoption without her knowledge or consent. Is this what happened or were they placed because Terri Hinson had abandoned them to run off to Charlotte with her boyfriend (Brittany's father), while she was married to Bryan Tripp, as Terry's own mother reported by letter, to Social Services?

The State of North Carolina failed to answer any of these and hundreds of other questions, and in so doing, doomed their case. The State of North Carolina v. Terri Louise Hinson, without being able to present a credible motive for the murder and attempted murder of her children would be asking a jury to believe the unbelievable: that a mother would kill her children. No amount of unequivocal expert testimony about Romex cables would ever convict Terri Hinson absent a compelling motive.

Ghosts Speak, But Only When Asked

The day after the fire, late Monday afternoon to be exact, this writer, upon learning from his Developmental Psychology students that their classmates, Terri and Rodney's house had burned and that infant Josh had died in the fire, drove from Southeastern Community College in Whiteville to Tabor City to offer help and support to Terri. During the trip, Coleman recalls the two or three times Terri had brought

Brittany and Josh to class, once each as part of the course requirement that each student bring a child to class as an example of developmental milestones, and once or twice bringing Josh, because she couldn't find anyone to babysit while she attended class. (Coleman had made, or had been persuaded by Terri to make, exceptions to the policy forbidding bringing children to class.)

Coleman's pained recall now fills with the images of Terri talking through her teeth to Josh, jerking him around, and relating to Josh as if he were not wanted. Coleman also remembers Josh's little wan face seeming so sickly, his nose emitting a thick mucus, and his orphaned clothes so different than those of his pert and pretty sister Brittany's... Josh's sad little face reminding Coleman of those little children various relief agencies use the media to solicit donations.

Not knowing where Terri would be, Coleman thinks to start with her neighbors. After getting directions to Wall St., Coleman arrives just as Rodney Strickland comes out of the house carrying a pair of boots and other items he is loading into a vehicle parked on the other side of the yellow crime scene police tape surrounding the property.

Unconcerned that he has just been caught violating the crime scene tape by his college professor, Rodney tells Coleman, "The fire started in an upstairs closet. The wires were bad." He then gives Coleman directions to Terri's mother house in Fair Bluff, some 15 miles away, but also right on the South Carolina border.

Spanish moss hangs from the water oaks lining the streets. The dead and dying center of this southern border town could be the set for a 40's "B" western, or the black and white classic, *The Last Picture Show*.

The beach-sand front yard is filled with cars. Coleman enters the screen porch across the front of the house and knocks. A hard, steely-eyed woman, 60-something, opens the door, and hearing Coleman ask for Terri, leads him through a suddenly dim hushed living room full of people, toward the back of the house, and a bedroom where a sobbing Terri is being embraced and comforted by an African-American female police officer.

Coleman takes his turn. Sitting on the bed, holding Terri in his arms, he answers her, "Why didn't I try to save my babies?" with, "Rodney says bad wiring caused the fire. You must have done all you could under the circumstances."

On his drive, back to Whiteville, Coleman cannot shake those images of baby Josh and Brittany – that beautiful little blond-haired-bright-eyed girl ... Sadness blurs the road. Later that night, as he tries to fall asleep, his gut would knot during replays of Terri's lament – her eerie, shrill – maybe even forced, tears. 'No,' he tells himself, 'poverty has a way of roughing up a mother's tenderness.'

He then remembers being in his office his first day at Southeastern Community College. His door is open. He looks up. Standing in the doorway, is a tall, hollow-cheeked, sandy-haired, tight-lipped, female wearing glasses, a loose shirt and jeans, and carrying a cigarette case. Looming behind, as if a detached shadow some 15 feet out in the foyer, is an adult male, maybe in his mid-to-late 40's. The female stretches her long thin arm out to shake hands, introduces herself as Terri Hinson, by saying, "I've heard you're the new Psyche Instructor. I'll be taking your courses. I just came by to check you out." With that, she turns and leaves.

Coleman would recall his uneasiness during that first encounter– the sense that Terri Hinson was sizing him up as to how to manipulate and control him -- the woman's steely coldness and control.

Two years later, June 1998, having been fired for questioning, at a faculty meeting, what the College President had done with the $374,000 the North Carolina Legislature had earmarked for faculty salaries, and for having charged that the signatures on ballots to elect faculty committee appointments had been forged to favor of friends of the College President, Coleman suddenly found himself unemployed and unemployable (Coleman finally figured out, that in the South, one never questions authority. NEVER.). He would also later learn that the College President had ordered a criminal justice student to do an illegal background check on Coleman. Information as to Coleman having been arrested for failing to return his daughter from visitation within 72 hours in violation of a civil Court Order, combined with his ex-wife's best friend having recently moved to town, with her claws still sharp, rendered Coleman free to freelance.

Since trying to console Terri the day after the fire, and going to Josh's funeral, Coleman had heard rumors from other students about Terri's arrest, the charges against her,

126

but his only contact with Terri while she was on "house arrest," was the time or two, she had barged into his class to demand information about her grades.   Sometime in mid-April or early May, 1998, a month before Coleman was axed, his students reported that the charges against Terry had just been dismissed. One student, in particular, Terri's former close friend, was put off by the dismissal, saying, "I know she did it."

So, beginning in June, 1998, Coleman began seeking an answer to the question: Was Terri Hinson a casualty of small town politics – the victim of a social caste system established 300 years ago to give the plantation owner absolute power and control over his Negroes? Or, had her arrest been a sexist demonstration of southern male's power over women? Or again, had she indeed murdered Josh just as Susan Smith, Diane, Downs, and Dr. Green murdered their children, but unlike them, had committed a mother's perfect crime?

In truth, Coleman admits that his experience after some 20 years living in the South and his recent encounter with what happens when one questions "The Main Man," – in that case, the College President – caused him to give his former student, Terri Hinson, the benefit of the doubt. In other words, he presumed – wanted to believe – she was innocent.

On July 14, 1998, Coleman interviewed Terri Hinson at her mother's home in Fair Bluff, North Carolina, where Terri, Brittany, and Terri's husband, Rodney Strickland were living. The interview took place at the kitchen table. Terri's mother was standing at the sink during most of the interview, occasionally attending to Brittany who was in and out. (Coleman would note the total absence of love and nurturing between the three generations of Hinson females.)

Terri gave her DOB as 4/24/64. She reported being the youngest of five siblings, two brothers and two sisters.

Justice for Baby Josh

One brother was killed in a car accident in 1991. Her father died of a heart attack in 1982. He had worked in a sewing plant. Her parents separated when Terri was 5. "I don't remember much about him. I had supervised visitation at my uncle's house. He did teach me how to fry sweet potatoes and how to check fish traps down in the river. He was kind of a loner. He was very abusive. He was a no-good-son-of-a-gun. Beat on me – my mother all the time. He was a non-drinker. His mother had 13 or 14 children. She didn't abuse her children. He didn't care about anybody but himself. My mother took him to court on assault charges – Harry Willis Hinson. He may have had a court record." (He did indeed) "He had a bad habit of staying up all night fussing and fighting. One time I told him not to wake me up. He grabbed me by the throat, but my sister, age 14, hit him over the head with a pot. We left him there. He fished illegally and sold the fish. He was jealous – wouldn't let me watch Perry Mason. Claimed I wasn't his. He was 19 years older than my mom. He had been married before. Abusive there too. Ricky, the brother who got killed in the car accident) was the only one who was close to him"

Terri recounted that her mother worked three jobs. Her father never paid any child support.

"I was accident prone – stitches twice. I was a tomboy. Fair Bluff Elementary School was heated by coal. I had Miss Boone and Miss Jenkins. I did OK, I really enjoyed school, except I fell and cut my head. At age 10, my mother remarried, so we had to move to Valdosta, Georgia, because his job transferred him. I didn't care one way or the other. I didn't get along. I didn't accept him. He was very quiet and on the road a lot, which didn't bother me. His name was Earl. He's dead, too. I didn't like having to ask him to do things. I did OK, until I turned 16, then I got rebellious, wild, and hanging with the wrong crowd. I ran away from home – just went down the road. Got locked up for B&E – broke into a

128

house myself. I just did it. I spent two days in jail. I straightened out. They put me on probation. I was bored in school. Began dating at 16. Moved to Wilmington, NC in the 10th grade. Began skipping school. School in Georgia had been real advanced. Wilmington put me in classes I already had. I stopped going. My worst class was Biology. Math was my best. Stayed in Wilmington only a few months. Earl gave up his own business and went back to work for his previous employer. We moved to Florence. I took a GED program, worked in an office waiting until my 18th birthday to join the navy.

My first husband, Bryan, lived across the street. He was very outgoing – fun. Our mothers had set up a blind date. We fought a lot when we dated, but not after we married. My mother said he had to join the Air Force – get a job before we could get married, so he did. I married at age 18. He went to boot camp. Three months later, my biological father died. Bryan was stationed in Tampa for a year. Earl had cancer, so we moved to Air Force base in Sumpter, South Carolina to be near my mother and step-father. Bryan got kicked out of the Air Force because of his weight and roll-backs. He got riffed. He had tried to kill himself with OD. I took him to the ER. I didn't feel sorry for him. I didn't love him – we were friends. I started reading typewriter ribbons and found love letters in a Beetle's Album. I confronted her. She was married.

I divorced him. We were moving in with my mom. He would get a job, and move out. My brother died (1991). My lung collapsed and Bryan moved to Whiteville working as a prison guard. We'd been together almost 8 years. We had three children, Bradley, born 2/84, Ashley born 12/26/ 87, and Timothy, born 11/10/88.

Bryan had been a wonderful father until the separation. He started drinking. Wouldn't pay child support. Didn't want visitation –pretty bad on kids, especially Bradley (the oldest), who was seven when we separated. We moved back in with my mother in Fair Bluff – three children and Bryant. He moved out in 1991.

I attended Horry Georgetown t Tech in Conway, SC, in phlebotomy. It was a quick course I needed for a quick job. Did rather well, but test for certification was only given at national sites and I didn't have the funds.

What happened next is confusing. I left kids with mom to go to Charlotte, January, 1991, and got a job in a laboratory killing monkeys for cultures. The smell was unbelievable.

I had already met Brittany's father before I went to Charlotte. His name was Phillip Williams. He was going to Charlotte. He moved in, started drinking, held me hostage for three days –he'd been drinking and doing "crack." He was determined I wouldn't go anywhere. I was pregnant (Brittany) I quit working at the lab because of chemicals and got a job at a real estate office. He was always threatening me with a knife – wild state of mind. He cut my arm and hand. I went to the ER. I reported him. I thought he would change. This was 1992. Brittany was born 9/10/92.

In October or November, I called the police with a black eye and bloody nose. They said it would only make him madder, so they refused to let me press charges. "Let him sober up," they told me. I would hide all the knives. I left him in Charlotte and came back to Fair Bluff. He followed me, stalked me, and threatened me. I moved out so he wouldn't hurt mom and then went with him to Conway. He worked off and on. He had been fired from a clothing store (alcohol & cocaine). In Conway, he was working for a rental company. One night, he beat me and threatened my boss's wife, so I left and came back to mom's in Fair Bluff. He started stalking me again. I'd call the Sheriff, but by the time they'd show up, he'd be back in South Carolina. This all happened in 1993-4.

I started at Southeastern Community College and he started following me to class. Brittany was at daycare in

South Carolina. He ran me off the road. I had a warrant on him in 1994. Phillip Gene Williams. He was "certified" crazy in South Carolina. He gets an SSDI check – goes to Columbia and checks himself in.

I entered the criminal justice program at Southeastern to find out how DSS could take my kids in 1992. Mom called Charlotte to tell me DSS was charging me with abandonment. Attorney Louis Sauls, who was representing the woman who had adopted Ashley, was Saul's secretary. I had only been gone to Charlotte 30 days. The day I came back, Sauls said I had no choice but to put the children for adoption or never see them again. Sauls told me to sign the adoption papers. I was never told I had a year to finalize the adoption or change my mind. I was told I needed $3,000 to pay a Charlotte attorney to take my case. I didn't find this out until I took courses in criminal justice at SCC.

I never saw my children again, except Timmy, (the youngest), who now lives here in Fair Bluff. He's the only one of the three I bonded with. It's been so long. I'm scared to uproot them. The oldest son, Bradley, is in Kentucky. I have no idea where the other one is. He wanted a dad to replace Bryan. My mother can see him, but I can't. I couldn't offer him anything. I had nothing. I don't know how he got taken – maybe a Baptist preacher in town is the connection. Bradley left in 1993.

I had Phillip's parental rights terminated. He'd told a social worker he wanted Brittany dead.

The fire? It took 48 minutes for Tabor City Fire Dept. to get Josh out. They killed him. They should have gone in through his bedroom window. Instead, they turned the hose on and steamed him to death."

Coleman continues his interview with Terri Hinson at her mother's house on July 17, 1998. She tells him, "I started as a teacher at SCC and then switched to criminal justice. I was a full-time student living with my mother. I moved to

Tabor City Apartments so Phillip Williams wouldn't hurt my mother. I dated Kenneth Bryant who I'd met at school. He was a good student – a girl student introduced us. He seemed ambitious, but I can't remember. He only stayed one quarter. He was a 4.0 student, but couldn't get financial aid because he'd made too much money the year before. He was 31 at the time. Born on New Year's Day. He had been previously married. His version of what happened to their marriage was that she was from a high-class family in Charlotte.

We dated 6-7 months. He went back on the road renovating motels. I found out I was pregnant. I was confused – how will I take care of it and go to school? His response? He wanted me to have an abortion. He took off and was never seen or heard from again, until I called his mother's house while I was in the hospital. He was there so I asked him if he wanted his name on the birth certificate. He said, "No." I hung up. Josh was born 5/10/95. Somebody added Kenneth's name to the birth certificate after the fire. I found out while in jail.

I met Rodney at SCC right before Josh was born. He was in criminal justice. He was separated. We dated. He moved in 6/1/96. She (Rodney's wife) started bar-hopping every night. She didn't see anything wrong. I tried to talk him into going back to her. They had two children, one a Marine, 21, and a son, 16, living with his mother. I expect to see him in a juvenile center soon. He's been arrested for drinking.

The week before the fire, I told Rodney – this is so routine; we do the same thing every day.

Josh was perfect child except he wouldn't talk. He was stubborn. Rodney was drawing Workman's Compensation. He'd been injured 2/94 at a chicken plant putting in steel beams. He slipped and fell across a steel beam on the ground below, injuring his lower back. He got a settlement of $20,000 a week after the fire. He was going to set up a kennel business but spent most of the settlement replacing lost items in the fire. He also paid off the car his oldest son had totaled.

On the night of the fire, 10/20/98, Sunday morning, they responded within minutes but took 48 minutes to get children out. They brought Brittany out first. Still bothers me a little. (Terri's glasses, cigarettes, and lighter are on the table. She sings while she goes to get a diagram of the house.). I had brought Brittany to mother's house. My mother brought Brittany home, we fed the kids. I plugged in the curling iron and fixed mother's hair. The iron was plugged in the living room behind the love seat. The space heater is an oil-filled electric heater and was also plugged in. It was made in Italy. The curling iron was on for 30 minutes. It was cold. Both heaters were on high – the one in the living room and the one upstairs. The curling iron stopped working. Both cords were hot – a lot of heat was coming. Rodney was at his mother's. I told my mom I would get Rodney to check the heater. I turned the curling iron back on and it worked ok. I finished mother's hair. I had put the kids to bed. She went home. The TV was on from a different outlet – the same one as the iron I used to iron clothes that night.

At 10:30 pm, Josh cried. I took a flashlight and went upstairs so not to wake the kids. There's no switch downstairs for upstairs lights. Josh was asleep. After Fran, lots of spiders came out. I flashed the light. No spiders. I went back downstairs. Finished ironing. Worked on Welbourne's history report. My brother Harry called around 10:30 -11:00, from Beaufort, SC, wanting us to help him move.

I decided to sleep on the couch to be there near the outlet in case anything happened. Both heaters were going and working fine. I was asleep on the couch. Brittany screamed, "Mommy, I'm scared!"

I saw the reddish/orange glow from stairs. I thought it was the heater upstairs caught fire. I ran to the stairs. One-quarter or one-half the way up, I saw fire coming from the top of the closet. (Josh's). I got to the top of stairs. Brittany is screaming. I yelled for her to run. She was in bed. I could see her in bed. I head to his room. The door blew out. I couldn't breathe. Got my hair singed. I made a U-turn toward Brittany's room. All black smoke. Couldn't see her. Just as black as could be. I couldn't breathe. Went downstairs to get the cordless phone and while calling went upstairs. Called 911. Got to top step, but heat and smoke.

Saw blue lights out front of the house. I ran downstairs with phone and opened door to tell them, "This is the house." Two officers ran in. One ran past me on way upstairs. he said, "I can't get in either room. I was thinking, they would get the kids. Now he was saying he couldn't. Two officers pulled me out of the house.

A fire truck arrived. I saw a man on the truck and pulled him off and brought him around to the back of the house to get a ladder to break a window to get Josh. He yelled for the ladder, got on, and yelled for some tool. He did not have his gear on.

Somebody pulled me away from the house. Gave me a coat to wear. I called Rodney and mom. I had speed dial. An officer took me across the street to neighbor's. The ambulance arrived when the fire engine came.

It never occurred to me what would happen to the kids – what fire would do (Terri laughs). I was in neighbor's house with Lt. Glenn. I kept asking him, "Where are my kids? Where are my kids?" He said, "Your daughter has gone to the hospital in Loris."
"What about my son?" He said they hadn't got him out yet. I asked him again. He told me both have been taken to the hospital. Then, he said I could go now.

As I went out of the house, Rodney pulled up in Mom's car. We went to the hospital in Loris, South Carolina, 7-8 miles away. Rodney drove me to the hospital. They wouldn't tell me anything.

Justice for Baby Josh

I called Betty Gore. She and her boyfriend Larry Stevens arrived. After about 30-40 minutes, the doctor said Josh didn't make it and Brittany was in critical condition. On the way, she died, CPR revived her. Over 40% carbon monoxide was in her blood –enough to kill an adult. They were going to airlift her to Charleston. Loris had forced oxygen into her. She was black, smoky, clammy feeling and not moving. I asked if I could go with her. They said, "No." Dr. Wright asked if I wanted to see Josh. I said "No." I preferred to remember him in his crib. (Terri became teary-eyed.) I stayed there until they flew Brittany out.

"We came to Mom's. I had to call the Funeral Home, Sunday morning 10:00 to 11:00. I kept calling Charleston Medical University and Rodney and I left for the hospital." (Coleman would be told during his investigation nearly two years later by a nurse at Brittany's hospital that no one from Brittany's family had called or visited by 6:30 PM on October 21, 1996. In fact, by the time Coleman had completed his six months' investigation, he would ascertain that almost every statement that Terri Hinson made during these two days of interviewing was misleading, distorted, or, most often, an outright lie.)

Terri went on to say, the hospital had Brittany tied down so she couldn't pull IVs and tubes out. They were going to keep her sedated so they could get her treated. (Terri is being very matter-of -fact, in control and talking fast, too fast, methinks.)

We kept going back and forth every day for 8 days except the day of the funeral that Wednesday. (Not according to the hospital and her friends, she didn't.)

I had heard on the news from Florence, SC, that Police Chief Wooster said the fire had been set. My brother Harry and Rodney said we had to take pictures. I thought they were wasting their time.

I went to Charleston to see Brittany. I attended a

135

staffing of some 12 doctors. I later found out while I was in jail that Police Chief Wooster had called to say I was under suspicion and that I should not be left alone with Brittany.

The day after the fire, a lady from Columbus DSS, Jennifer Baldwin came to the Wall St. house, where I gave her a statement. She said, "It looks to me as if you're being set up." (Not according to Jennifer Baldwin's transcript.)

I went to the hospital for the staffing. They said they had told Brittany nothing about the fire. Thursday, I told her Josh had died, and that she wasn't to get upset. She was still coughing and her throat sounded scratchy. (This would have been four days after the fire.) She was having nightmares.

On Friday, Day 5, I was told I could not take her off the floor to play or visit. They said DSS and Chief Wooster had instructed them. (Would Jennifer Baldwin have believed Terri had been "set up" and still issued such a watch order? (Not hardly.) They were always checking on us while I was with Brittany.

Brittany said, "I want my little Josh. Jesus came to get Josh." Brittany's little face was wet with tears. She suddenly wiped her face and said, "I'm not going to cry anymore."

Monday, DSS came to Charleston and said they wanted to talk to us. Dr. Bryan Maynor was there at a long table. Brittany's psychologist was there. DSS said they were taking custody of Brittany. Dr. Maynor started crying and said, "You're making a mistake." I asked for grounds, but said, "to heck with it." I thought I could fight it later. DSS said they were taking Brittany to a foster home. Dr. Maynor said, "1 You're making a mistake. This is 3-4 in the afternoon. I was told to explain it to Brittany, but not to get upset.

It was tough. I did it without crying. DSS came to the room to get her stuff. They told me to leave. I broke down in the hall as I was leaving. (Terri cries.)

I called my lawyer. "They took her" I saw my attorney the next day. I was staying with Mom, so I had to move out so Mom could get custody. At the hearing, Mr. Holt got custody for Mom, where Brittany stayed until Mom had a stroke on January 2, 1998.

I was given twice-a-week visitation. Mrs. Baldwin, who quit DSS in the middle of the case, now works for the Health Dept. in Columbus County. At first, she was quite cautious. Scared to say anything. She knew she'd messed up.

I saw Brittany twice a week. I rented a house a few miles down the road in South Carolina. Brittany needed a check-up in Lumberton. I asked if I could take her.

On the way back, (November 20, 1996) we saw Matt White, from the SBI on the side street next to Mom's. He got out of his car as I pulled up and said, "I have three warrants for your arrest. He was in plain clothes. and didn't handcuff me. He had a female agent with him.

The night before, November 19, 1996, Matt White had come by the house to ask Brittany if she could light a cigarette lighter. Brittany wouldn't have anything to do with him. He tried to get her to light it. She said, "No, it will hurt me."

He took me to the Sheriff's Dept. Matt White couldn't do the fingerprints. I had to tell him to roll my prints. He says if I tell him Brittany did it, it will all be over." I said, "There's no way in hell I'd do it. There's no way I'd let her grow up thinking she's done something like this." I told him they could arrest her for murder and arson when she turns 18. He said, "The truth will set you free." I said, "It certainly will in this case," He asked if I would waive my Miranda Rights. I said, "No. I think you just arrested me for murder and arson. I need a lawyer."

The next morning, they arraigned me in jail. The Judge came to the jail. Judge Aldridge, who said he was appointing Craig Wright as my attorney. I'd paid the rent to Attorney Richard Wright the morning of the fire. Judge Aldridge couldn't set bail because of the murder charge and I was being bound over to a Grand Jury.

I spent 61 days in jail in Whiteville. The girls there were supportive – fighting bad checks charges and child support. They were wonderful. Christmas was the toughest. One stayed six months. They kept putting their court dates off. One woman was arrested for murder in Texas 20 years ago. Her charges were dropped.

My lawyer came several times a week to see me. I trusted attorney Bill Wood. If he'd been my original attorney none of this would have gone as far as it did. Craig Wright refused to let me appear at the Grand Jury.

My first Bond Hearing before Judge Gore was continued because I couldn't answer and document a juvenile arrest record, etc.

Over Christmas break, I got copies of the Discovery package. At the second Bond Hearing on January 15, 1997, I made them look like idiots. Someone had said I came out of the house that night wearing a jacket, when the jacket was a coat given me by the rescue squad.

Bond was set at $200,000 and I was placed under house arrest. It took all Mom's savings and eight bondsmen to do it.

I lived with my sister and Rodney in a mobile home. My sister Linda sold her home and land in Charlotte and rented the mobile home. I requested visitation with Brittany 2 days/week for two hours each. She would try to get it all in. It was sad. Brittany called me every night. Huge phone bills

Jennifer Baldwin began easing up and later admitted, "I made a mistake, but don't know how to get out of it."

I was sending Rodney everywhere to get law books. This was all wrong. Attorneys weren't doing anything. Then, I got a computer in September, 1997, and started reviewing the file piece by piece in preparation for the trial because I wasn't going into the courtroom with my first chair attorney. He didn't do anything. He (Craig Wright) had the Discovery

File for 8 months and hadn't read it. He said he always waits until a month before trial to read the prosecution's file, "so I won't forget."

Mary Ann Talley, an attorney in Raleigh, reviews all capital cases in North Carolina. She tells attorneys to do a Daubert Motion. Attorney Craig Wright did not know the case. Every expert witness must represent a consensus of the experts in that field. When I asked if he would do a Daubert Motion, he said, "No." My sister Ann called him and threatened to go to the newspapers if my attorney didn't do something on the case. This was in February and March, 1988, or 1 ½ years after the fire. He called me and told me to "calm Ann down."

In October, I had contacted Dr. Hurst through the Internet (But your sister insisted in a letter to your attorney that she had found Dr. Hurst.) and for months he and I began sending e-mails back and forth, advising me what to do. He's a chemist.

My attorney had told me not to communicate with anyone, so my sister Lynn contacted Dr. Hurst asking him to contact the attorney so Dr. Hurst could come into the case. My attorney refused. to bring him in. I said, "Why aren't you going to use Dr. Hurst?" My attorney answered, "What does a chemist know about a fire investigation?" He kept stalling until my sister Ann threatened him.

Dr. Hurst and Ken Gibson, fire investigators, came here around March 24, 1998, to look at the fire scene. SBI Agent Matt White was outside the house all day as part of the Court Order. They stayed all week. I burned the fire investigator's steaks. They went with DA Bollinger, along with our fire investigator Wyman Sox, from Columbia, South Carolina. Matt White didn't show that afternoon. Dr. Hurst cross-examines using White's evidence. The DA dismissed the case on April 17th. It had been a very long 18 months. I learned:

1. Don't trust Columbus County; they broke every law in the book.

2. I don't trust the law at all. It's like this everywhere – people being arrested for things they hadn't done.

3. They based their case on SBI Agent's testimony. All they had to do is have him say I started the fire, therefore that's all they needed to arrest me.

Matt White has no background as arson investigator that can be found. He's not listed with any fire investigation association.

Before I found Dr. Hurst, I couldn't trust anyone. If I hadn't gotten the computer and got on-line, I'd be in on Death Row.

I believe my attorney wanted to see me convicted. He was in cahoots or related to Richard Wright, (Coleman's genealogical study determined Craig Wright and Richard Wright were at best so distant, their lineage could not be traced, if it did indeed exist.) So if they convicted me, the landlords are off the hook in terms of wrongful death negligence and so is the insurance company, USF&G, for having insured property not up to code and failure to warn their insured. Insurance Company USF&G had inspected the property 4-5 days before the fire and needed to see me convicted. The Columbus County Building Inspector had approved the wiring done previously so he needs me convicted, too.

I spent 61 days in the Columbus County Jail. Scary. The capacity is 8, but they had up to 30 at one time. One cell for women. No exercise. No outside. On Christmas day, I got to stand outside. I saw one fight. This crazy black girl and white lesbian – I wrote a warning. The black girl was ignoring racial comments by the white girl, who had already been caught with a weapon – a real trouble-maker. A fight broke out. Black girl won. She wouldn't stop til they pulled them away.

Justice for Baby Josh

The bathroom is right there in the cell. The assumption is you'd had to have done something wrong to be in jail, so the conditions are supposed to be bad... 61 days of crying, anger, and hurt. Scared.

I could have seen Brittany, but I didn't want her to see me. Had visits Saturday and Sunday, in visitor's room.

My absolute lowest was when I was losing the baby, January, 1998. I'm high-risk pregnancy – three miscarriages and one stillborn. Nurses at the Health Department sent me to the high-risk clinic. The Doctor said, "We'll wait a while." I was under house arrest There's no doctor. I was having spotting. I called. They said to stay off my feet. I kept calling. December, 1997, I finally go to Health Department. I went to the ER for an ultrasound. The Dr. refused and sent me home. Pregnancy test showed I was still pregnant. The next day, there was a lot of bleeding. I was sent back to the hospital for ultrasound. When I got home, the Health Department called and said, "The baby was dead," and I had to have surgery to remove the fetus (Terri shows no tears or emotion.). The PA gave me a prescription for Xanax. Knocked me out. Never took any more. I didn't know where I was at.

Every time I turned around, they were taking something from me. Patricia Sanderson, Intensive Probation, felt bad about what had happened, but couldn't do anything about it. Why hadn't Wilmington, which had my file, called the Health Department?

Coleman noted that during the several hours of interviewing Terri Hinson in her mother's home on two different days and observing three generations of Hinson females interacting with one another, he was struck by the absence of warmth, affection, or spontaneity. Indeed, grandmother, mother, and daughter spoke to each other as if they were meeting for the first time, or perhaps as if theirs was a business relationship, with grandmother being the director of the daycare, Terri Hinson, her manager, and

Brittany, their new, and only client.

Coleman reported he never once saw any hugging, smiling, laughing, or signs of trust – A family strange and estranged, drawn together only out of the necessity of defending themselves against all non-family members, while at the same time being vigilant that the other two didn't betray the third.

The lack of interactive love and bonding aside, Coleman was troubled that Brittany seemed destined to continue the Hinson family's inability to trust, and therefore to love and bond, resulting in Brittany bringing children into the world who might also become victimized.

Finally, Coleman was unsettled by his former student's attempt to sell him on the idea that she didn't murder Josh when a simple sign of genuine grief would have rendered such saleswoman-ship redundant.

Finally, there appeared to be glaring contradictions in Terri Hinson's statements which could not be attributed to the 20 months which had elapsed between the fire on October 20, 1996, and the interview in July, 1998. For example, Terri Hinson claimed that it took 48 minutes for the firemen to bring Brittany and Josh out of the house, which if true, Brittany would certainly have died in the fire. Second, Terri seemed to be belaboring the issue of a having decided to sleep downstairs because of her concern over the downstairs heater – a concern which she seemed to have contrived. If she had indeed been that worried about the downstairs heater, why didn't she simply use the existing baseboard heating system, or go to bed upstairs where she had placed that heater in the hall so as to heat the three bedrooms? In fact, at one point, she claimed she had shut the door to Josh's bedroom due to "excessive heat," which meant there was more than enough heat upstairs for her bedroom. Third, if she were concerned about keeping her children safe and warm, why not have them in bed with her? Or, spend the night at her mother's until the supposed electrical problems had been fixed? Fourth, she told Coleman that "one-fourth-to-one-half way up the stairs, I saw fire coming the top of (Josh's) closet." But she had already said she had been awakened to a "reddish/orange glow" coming all the way down to the bottom of the stairs in the living room. How would it be possible for the fire's reflection to turn the corner in Josh's bedroom, be strong enough to travel the full length of the hallway, travel down the stairs, and yet allow her to still climb the stairs while not complaining of the fire's heat? Another apparent contradiction was that Terri Hinson told Coleman that when she went upstairs, "I could see her (Brittany) in bed. I yelled for her to run." If she could see Brittany, why didn't she rescue her? Why would she tell Brittany, "Run?" Run, rather than, "Get down and crawl as fast as you can to Mommy," who should have been reaching toward her daughter with pleading out-stretched arms? Run? Too strange! As if contrived afterward to explain why she did so little to save her children?

After interviewing his former student Terri Hinson at her mother's residence on two separate occasions, Coleman went to the Tabor City Police Department to review police reports and interview the officers who were present at the fatal fire on October 20, 1996.

Coleman was first struck with the unanimity of the officers that Terri Hinson had set the fire and that she had gotten by with murdering her infant son, attempted murder of her daughter and arson because the SBI had basically snubbed the local police, who had been eye-witnesses to Terri Hinson's erratic behavior during the fire.

For example, Officer Moyer, who, according to his report, arrived at the fire at "0358 hours" found "female subject standing in the door, fully dressed, holding a cell phone and yelling, "My babies are upstairs!" As Moyer rushed up the stairs he saw flames UNDER the door, "straight ahead," meaning Josh's bedroom door was closed. There would be only one reason why Josh's bedroom was closed: To make certain he died. Officer Moyer's statements raise these questions: (1) Why was Terri Hinson sleeping fully dressed at 3:58: AM on Sunday morning? (2) Why was she standing in the doorway instead of trying to save her children? (3) Why was Josh's bedroom door closed, when Terri Hinson had recounted to Coleman that she had a space heater turned on as the only source of heat for the three upstairs bedrooms on the night of the fatal fire? If Josh's room had become excessively warm so that she closed his door, why didn't she simply turn the heater down or off, rather than leaving it on "high" and closing his door? When did she close his door? She claimed not to have gone upstairs again after checking on Josh, who she alleged cried out around 10:30? How could she claim to have seen flames "whooshing" out of Josh's closet if his door was closed? She had to have left the door open while the fire got started and then closed it to trap Josh inside the inferno.

Officer Russell, who had arrived seconds before Moyer, could see "smoke coming from the top of the house and the windows were black from smoke. He and officer Moyer "were met at the door of 101 Wall Street by Terry Hinson," who told us that "her children were upstairs and that she was unable to get them. Mrs. Hinson was on the phone and very upset at the time of our arrival." After being turned back by the smoke at the top of the stairs, the officers ran around to see if there was another entrance to the house. Finding none, they returned to the front, at which time Officer Moyer instructed "Mrs. Hinson to get out of the house." Then Officer Russell tried again to go up the stairs to rescue the children. "All I could see was an orange light under the door straight ahead. The house was exited at that time by patrolman Moyer, Mrs. Hinson, and I. At 0359 the first fire truck arrived, followed by Corporal Gause."

Officer Russell reported "smoke coming from the top of the house and the windows (upstairs) were black with smoke," meaning no signs of flames. If neither of the officers arriving on the scene saw any sign of flames from the upstairs windows, how could Terri Hinson have seen "a reddish-orange glow from the stairs" reflected at the bottom of the stairway from where she was sleeping on the couch across the living room? Furthermore, both Officers Russell and Moyer, in separate trips up the stairs to rescue the children, independently reported seeing "orange light under the door straight ahead." Again, if the officers did not notice any sign of flames until they reached a place on the stairs where they could see under the bedroom door straight ahead, how could Terri Hinson have seen "fire coming from top of closet" in Josh's bedroom, as she claimed in her interview with Coleman, when Josh's bedroom door was closed? How could Terri Hinson have known the fire was in Josh's closet unless she set it there?

Officer Annie Gause reports when she arrived on the scene, she observed Officers Russell and Moyer "escorting a w/f from the residence. (Terri Hinson had told Coleman that the officers had to "pull" her away from the house, implying she was still trying to go back in to rescue her children.)" ...the W/F stated she had checked the upstairs base heater earlier and had closed the children's doors because of the excessive heat. (Instead of closing their bedroom doors, why not just turn the heater down or off? No one ever reported Brittany's door to be closed.) She had the fallen asleep on the sofa downstairs, until being awoken when she smelled a strong odor of smoke. (Hinson told everyone else, it was Brittany calling, "Mommy, I'm scared," that awoke her and when she did, she saw reddish/orange flames reflected in the stairway.) She then jumped up and ran upstairs to the bedroom directly at the top ... She then stated that she looked at the heater and it was fine because it was hot before. After doing this, she opened the door to Jason's (Josh's) room and was overcome by the flames, which appeared to be coming from the closet. As she opened the door, the pressure closed it, which burned her hair." (How could Hinson have seen the glow of the flames at the bottom of the stairs and from the sofa on which she had been sleeping, if Josh's bedroom door had been closed?)

According to Officer Gause, at this time, W/F began yelling, 'Get my babies! You don't understand; I lost two children before. My boyfriend will kill me!'

Trooper John Lewis, the next door neighbor, asked W/F to come over to his house. As she was leaving, "a firefighter came toward me carrying a small W/F child, which appeared to (be) lifeless and very gray in color." The child was placed into the rescue vehicle and transported to Loris Community Hospital. I then advised Central to send a second Rescue unit. A second firefighter approached carrying a small semi-blackened child, who was placed in the second Rescue unit to be taken to Loris Community Hospital. "The next thing that occurred was the mother, Mrs. Hinson, being escorted to a vehicle by a W/M, identified as Rodney Strickland, Mrs. Hinson's boyfriend, who left for the hospital.

While the Gause report called Josh "Jason" and makes no mention as to why Terri Hinson did not request, nor ride with either of her children, Officer Gause does note that the mother did, in fact, wait for her boyfriend, rather than riding in the ambulance with either of her severely injured children.

In his report, Tabor City Police Lt. Glenn wrote that Terri Hinson told him that she "had placed a heater upstairs to keep the children warm ...that the plug-in heater downstairs, continuously got hot to the touch when plugged in. She heard her daughter crying ...when she reached the top of the stairs, she saw a flash and flames... the fire came from the direction of the closet area of her son's room. She ran downstairs and called 911. "I noticed Ms. Hinson's hair was burned and scorched and her face was red and (?) looking... She stated someone told her the fire was electrical and caused by the heater upstairs, but that the fire came from the child's closet. She would be on her way to the hospital as soon as her mother arrived."

Lt Glenn called Officer Ramey, who had rented the house prior to Terri Hinson. Ramey told Lt Glen that the circuit breaker "kept switching off, a lot of the outlets didn't work, and most of the switches were loose and in need of replacement. Ramey had no problems with sparks or heated wires. Ramey recalled buying four smoke detectors and placing them throughout the house. There were none present at the time of the fire.

At 0730 hours, Corporal Gause called to say there were subjects in the Wall Street residence. Officer Russell drove to the scene to find Rodney Strickland and Terri Hinson had crossed the crime scene police tape and were in the house removing items. Officer Gause advised Strickland and Hinson to meet Chief Wooster and Lt. Glen at the police station. At the station, Hinson told Lt. Glenn that she had slept downstairs because she was concerned that the electrical plug on the heater would spark or cause a problem and that the wire felt hot earlier. She added she did not know how the fire could have started in the closet as there were no electrical boxes or panels in the room. She volunteered she had three children who had been "taken and adopted." She further stated that the "door to the bedroom was always open and she didn't know how the door (Josh's bedroom) could have closed. She acknowledged that this door was "extremely hard to open and close. Ms. Hinson told Lt. Glenn she was "on (welfare) support, but claimed to own both vehicles, including a Mustang parked to the right side of the house." As part of his investigation, Lt. Glenn reported that Terri Hinson had a record of "bad checks," an arrest record as a juvenile, and as having left Josh in the car while she attended classes at Southeastern Community College. Before moving to 101 Wall Street in Tabor City, she and Rodney had lived at the Tabor Villa Apartments, where Terri wrote the apartment manager, she would be breaking the lease because, "I have a deteriorating bone condition and can't go up the stairs." (Of course, the 101 Wall Street rental has all three bedrooms upstairs, including Terri Hinson's bedroom and the only bathroom.)

From these police reports and interviews. Coleman learned that each and every officer independently stated they were absolutely certain Terri Hinson set the fire. Coleman's evidence to support the police's conclusion includes, but is not limited to the following:

1. Terri Hinson was fully dressed, including shoes and socks, wearing glasses, carrying her cigarette case, and talking on the phone when Officers Russell and Moyer arrived at the fire. If she was dressed at the time she first became aware of the fire, was that because she had to be ready to jump ship as soon as the fire had done its treachery and before she became a victim herself? Was she making sure her most important personal possessions were not damaged in the fire, namely herself, her glasses, her cigarettes, and her phone? If she dressed AFTER finding out the house was on fire, why didn't she try to save her children before securing her possessions and herself?

2. Both Officers Russell and Moyer reported the upstairs windows to be completely black. If there were no signs of flames, Terri Hinson could not have seen a "reddish/orange glow" in the stairway down into the living room where she had been sleeping on the couch across the room. If there were no signs of flames in the upstairs when Officer Russell and Moyer arrived at the fire, Josh's bedroom door was closed, and his mother could not have known the fire was in Josh's closet, unless that had been where she set

the fire.

2. Both Officer Moyer and Officer Russell independently reported seeing flames under Josh's closed bedroom door as they tried to climb the stairs to try to rescue him, but were turned back by the heavy smoke. In her statement to Lt. Glenn, Terri Hinson had acknowledged that Josh's bedroom door was "extremely hard to open and close." By her admission, the only person strong enough to close Josh's bedroom door was his mother, Terri Hinson, and the only reason to close the door, was to make certain that her son Josh died in the fire.

3. Terri Hinson claimed she was sleeping downstairs because she was concerned about the perceived danger caused by the downstairs space heater, when the obvious solution would have been to use the safe baseboard electric heat and sleep upstairs in her own bed. An equally obvious remedy to the questionable safety of the downstairs heater, would have been to use only the upstairs heater which she placed in the hall so as to heat the three upstairs bedrooms, including her own. At another time, she told Lt. Glen she had shut the "children's bedroom doors because of excessive heat," meaning the upstairs heater produced more than enough heat for the three bedrooms, and therefore, it had been unnecessary to sleep downstairs in the first place. The only reason for her to be sleeping downstairs fully clothed, including her shoes, was so she could be sure to get out of the house in time, once the fire was burning sufficiently to kill Josh and Brittany.

4. At various times, Terri Hinson told the police the children's doors were "always open," at another time, "I closed the children's doors because of excessive heat" (from the space heater), another time, "I don't know why the door (Josh's bedroom) was closed, and then later, explained that the fire itself, to wit, the pressure of the fire, caused Josh's door to close, even if she had also told the police, Josh's

149

bedroom door was "extremely hard to open or close."

Only if she were lying, would she so blatantly contradict herself and her story, and only if she were guilty of murder, attempted murder, and arson, would Terri Hinson need to be lying.

5. Terri Hinson told police she was awakened by Brittany's crying, but also claimed she was awakened by the smell of smoke. It would seem more likely that she was awake downstairs waiting for the fire to do its mission, rehearsing her story, and calling 911 as soon as she was convinced her children were dead.

6. Terri Hinson told Officer Gause that when she opened the door to Josh's bedroom (thereby admitting the door had been closed), "I was overcome by the flames which appeared to be coming from the closet," If she were standing in the door with flames leaping out at her, how could she know the source of the flames to be a closet at the opposite corner of the room, unless she had set the fire there?

7. Terri Hinson told Lt. Glenn she heard her daughter crying and went up to check on her, that when she reached the top of the stairs, she saw a "flash and flames" coming from the closet area of her son's bedroom." She told officer Gause it had been the smell of smoke which had awakened her, and another officer, that she saw a "reddish/orange glow on the stairway.

How could she have seen a "flash of flames" when she reached the top of the stairs if the door was closed as she admitted it was? Again, how, from the top of the stairs, could she see across the hall and into her son's closet in the far-left corner, even if the door were open and there were no flames in her face? Why, if the smell of smoke was strong enough to wake her, did Terri Hinson need to go up the stairs to "check" on her daughter? Why, if she had seen a "reddish/orange glow" emanating from the stairway, did she not conclude there was a fire upstairs, call 911 and rush to save her children?

The only plausible answer to these questions, even allowing for police reporting margin of error, is that Terri Hinson was lying to cover to her arson, murder, and attempted murder.

8. Terri Hinson proclaimed to both Officer Gause and Lt. Glenn that, "I already lost two children" (Gause) "3 children (Glenn) My boyfriend (Rodney Strickland) will kill me." (Why? None of these were Rodney's. Besides, friends had heard Rodney say he had already raised two children of his own and didn't want to be raising someone else's.

Coleman's interpretation is that Terri Hinson, in a desperate attempt to convince the police of her grief, conjures an explanation which would have been superfluous had her sorrow been genuine, but so out of context as to have the opposite effect of arousing suspicion. First, as she later told Coleman, the children were not "lost," but rather put up for adoption by Terri Hinson. Second, they were born and adopted years before she met Rodney Strickland. (Faced with getting rid of their children or losing their boyfriend, Susan Smith, and Diane Downs, also chose to murder their children.)

Thus, in her contrived excuse for feeling grief, she admitted her guilt and her motivation. The smoking gun was in plain view but unseen by the State of North Carolina due to male bias of forensic myopia.

9. Everyone at the scene of the fire agreed that Terri Hinson never tried to see either Brittany or Josh as they were each brought out of the house by the firemen. They all noted that Terri Hinson never asked to ride in the ambulance with either Brittany or Josh, and in fact, told police, firefighters, and ambulance personnel, that instead, she would wait for her boyfriend, which she did.

In this writer's view, this single act of egregious callousness instructs us as to Terri Hinson's motivation. By this monstrous demonstration of her "Susan Smith" preference for her boyfriend over her children, Terri Hinson should have signed her own death warrant. But again, the SBI chose to pursue only physical evidence, and in so doing, blew the investigation, lost their case, and failed to obtain justice for Josh and the citizens of Columbus County.

Terri Hinson's actions, behavior, and statements, while unconscionable and reprehensible in the context of a mother's relationship with her children, can only make sense if Terri Hinson believed the only way she was ever going to get Rodney Strickland and his Workmen's Compensation Settlement was to get rid of her children. There was no other way.

10. Police, firefighters, and ambulance staff all noted independently of one another, that at no time did they observe Terri Hinson crying or sobbing. Yelling, yes. Upset, yes. But, tears, grief, or heartbreak, no. If she had accomplished her goal of killing Josh but had to seem to the police as if she were sad, is it not easier to yell, shout, and act upset, than to fake crying inconsolably? Of course, it is. Especially in a person so callous, calculating, and without conscience or remorse.

11. Lt. Glenn was the only one who reported that Terri Hinson's hair was singed and her face flushed. There were no other signs of her skin or clothing having been burned. There are three possible explanations. One, she did, in fact, go up the stairs during the fire, most likely to see if the fire had progressed sufficiently to close Josh's bedroom door. Two, she singed her hair while setting the fire. Three, she deliberately singed her hair on the curling iron she admits to having used earlier that night.

12. At one point, Terri Hinson, yelled, "My little boy is dead." Josh had yet to be brought out. She could not have known he was dead unless she had seen him dead in his crib before she shut his door.

13. Terri Hinson told Lt. Glenn the fire started in Josh's closet when no one had told her that's where it started. So how did she know unless that's where she started the fire?

14. Three hours after Brittany had been airlifted to the Charleston Children's Burn Center and three hours after Josh had been declared DOA, Officer Gause sees Terri Hinson and Rodney Strickland crossing the yellow crime scene tape removing items from the burned residence. Why wasn't the grieving mother in Charleston at her dying daughter's bedside? She claimed she was taking video tapes to Brittany, but in fact, she did not show up in Charleston until days later. Hmmm.

Coleman interviewed Corporal Brian Ramey, Tabor City policeman, who had rented the 101 Wall Street just prior to Terri Hinson and Rodney Strickland. Ramey stated he had purchased four smoke detectors from Sam's or Wal-Mart in Fayetteville. "I installed one in the kitchen, one in the living room, one in the hallway upstairs, and one in the master bedroom. The carpet in the bedroom at the head of the stairs (Josh's room) was "very thick," making it hard to open or close the door. The house was drafty and cold."

Neither the police, the SBI, nor fire investigators found smoke detectors in the house at the time of the fire.

Coleman interviewed State Trooper Jon Lewis and his wife, Jamie Lewis, who were Terri Hinson's only neighbors, in that the side of the Lewis residence is across the street, and up from the Hinson rental, which is the only house on that block.

Trooper Lewis recounted that the emergency vehicle sirens had awakened him around 4:00 AM. Looking out his upstairs bathroom window, he saw fire coming from the rear of the Hinson house. When he arrived on the scene, he saw Terri Hinson standing outside with a Tabor City police officer. As Lewis approached, both the officer and Terri

Hinson told Trooper Lewis that the children were still inside. Terri Hinson seemed very upset but was not crying. She did say, "I don't know why I couldn't get my babies." (Coleman would note that Terri would repeatedly volunteer "I don't know," as a way to seemingly answer an impugning question before it was asked.)

Trooper Lewis invited Terri to come over to his house and then returned home to tell his wife that Terri may be coming over. Some time later, Terri accompanied by his wife Jamie, entered the Lewis home, where Hinson was interviewed by a Tabor City officer. Trooper Lewis said he and his wife had had little or no contact with either Terri Hinson or the adult male occupant. Lewis had been told that the male was married to a woman who lived in Fair Bluff with their children. Trooper Lewis said that a private investigator had questioned him about the man living with Terri in regard to a Workmen's Compensation claim, in which the man (Rodney Strickland) was unable to work. Trooper Lewis said that he had seen the man mowing the lawn and doing odd jobs around the house which seemed to require strenuous effort. Trooper Lewis recalled that before he went to work at 8:00 AM on the morning of the fire, he saw the man living with Terri Hinson cross the crime scene yellow tape to remove clothing and other items from the house and put them in the silver Cougar parked in the driveway. "I don't remember the time her boyfriend arrived.

My wife Jamie said Terri seemed upset, but not as upset as a mother would be if her children were inside a burning house. We both wondered why she was standing outside instead of trying to save her children. Everyone in town thinks she did it."

For her part, Jamie Lewis said that about 10 minutes after her husband had gone over to see if he could help at the scene of the fire, he returned to ask her to get dressed because Terri may be coming over. Shortly after her husband left,

Terri arrived with a Tabor City police officer, who she sat with during his interview of Terri. Jamie Lewis recalled Terri telling the officer (Lt. Glenn) that she fell asleep downstairs because of some electrical heater she didn't trust. She awoke when she heard her little girl crying, and that when Terri heard a "whoosh: sound, she knew the house was on fire. Terri told the officer that she went upstairs to check on the upstairs heater, it was ok. Jamie Lewis remembered that Terri "repeatedly stated that her son was such a pretty little boy, that she could not believe that she had lost him." Jamie Lewis reported that Terri was not crying or "hysterical," but only upset. Terri's hair was singed, but there were no signs that her clothing had burned, or that she had been injured, She did have a cordless phone in her hand, but was not wearing her glasses. After the interview was completed, the officer left and five minutes later, Terri asked to go back outside. It was about 4:30 am. Outside, Jamie and Terri met a woman, Jamie assumed was Terri's mother and a man, she assumed was Terri's father. The woman asked Terri about the children. Terri responded, "No one will tell me anything." A Tabor City police officer approached and offered Terri assistance. Terry asked to see her children. The officer told her they had been taken to the hospital in Loris, South Carolina. Terri then asked if she could go to the hospital and was told, "Of course." Terri left with the man and the woman.

Jamie Lewis said that was the only time she had ever spoken to Terri Hinson other than once before when she had asked Terri if she could play with the dog because it was chained up all day and nobody ever played or paid attention to the dog.

Volunteer Fireman Jeff Fowler, who found Josh in his crib, told Coleman, "The door to the boy's bedroom was shut. No one had tried to get into his room before I did. She (Terri Hinson) had not tried to get to the boy." Fowler had written in his report, that when he arrived on the scene, "The house had

155

power. A living light was on, and the firemen had trouble pulling the electrical meter box from the base."

Tracey Fowler, the volunteer fireman who rescued Brittany, reported that when he reached the top of the stairs, he did not see any flames. When he heard a cry to his left, he dropped to his knees and began crawling in the direction of the cry. His knees struck something. Then, he felt legs and a head just inside the doorway, heading toward the bed as if she had been trying to crawl under the bed. He picked up the child to his chest and then walked out on his knees. Once outside, he handed the child to a rescue worker and went back inside to look for the second child.

A few days later, he returned Terri Hinson's call. She asked where he had found Brittany. She then began talking about all the damage the fire had caused. Fowler recalled she did not seem upset, but sounded nervous and was talking very fast. She said "Thank you," and hung up.

Was the call a ruse to find out what Fowler knew and what he might say to blow the lid off Terri Hinson's claim that she had told Brittany to "run." Indeed, if Terry Hinson had seen Brittany in her bed and told her to "run," why didn't Brittany's mother try to help her daughter? If Brittany had been told to "run," why was she found only four feet from the door, face down, trying to crawl under her bed for safety? Or, is the only truth that Terri heard Brittany cry, "Mommy, I'm scared," but did nothing, leaving her four-year-old daughter to try to save herself by crawling under her bed, while her mother waited downstairs trying to calculate the latest possible time to call 911, without arousing suspicion, yet allowing enough time for the fire to kill her children?

Coleman obtained a copy of the following statement volunteered by The Tabor City Rescue Squad:

On the early Sunday morning of October the 10th, 1996, Tabor City Rescue Squad responded to a structure fire that claimed two lives. One hour later, the same crew responded to a sick call, and as they returned to the station, the pages sounded for yet another structure fire. But this call was one that will be remembered for a long time.

As we got out of 2105 and headed to the bay doors to leave our station, Gary Sykes made the comment about smelling smoke and then the pages sounded once again. When the call came across our pages, the 911 Dispatcher advised us that it was yet another structure fire, but this time children were trapped inside.

The address was given to go to Wall Street and the time en route was 03:58 and at 03:59, 2105 was 10-23 right behind 404 (Annie Gause). Upon our arrival, the mother met us in the road, screaming to us that we made her leave her babies. The mother was fully dressed, carrying a cordless phone, cigarette case, and wearing her glasses, and her hair was minor sieged (singed) around the edge.

The Tabor City Fire Department arrived seconds behind the ambulance, all within two minutes of receiving the call. As we stood there in horror, you could see the fire blazing through the window in front of us. Gary Sykes who was the driver of 2105 helped fireman Gary Watts, a Tabor City Fireman, get a ladder up to the front window of 101 Wall Street, to the window where the mother said her children were at. Tabor City officers had already tried to go up the stairs from the kitchen but the dining room table was up against the door. Due to heavy smoke, they (the officers) had to come out.

As the firemen went up the ladders, the ambulance (staff) was trying to get information from the mother, but she was steady calling people on the cordless telephone. When we did find out that they (there?) were two children, Lorrie Lancaster called Columbus Central, our Dispatcher, and asked for an additional ambulance. Lorrie also asked the mother to get in the front seat, because when the children were located, we would be going to the hospital. She said she had to wait for her boyfriend.

At 04:06 the first child was found by fireman Tracey Fowler. She was located on the upstairs bedroom floor in the prone position beside of her bed. As the fireman rushed out with the four-year-old lifeless child in his arms, he handed her to Gary Sykes, who put her on the stretcher inside the ambulance. The mother was asked to ride with us, but again she said she had to wait on her boyfriend.

Upon the assessment, we found the little girl with a very slow pulse and only breathing three times a minute. An oropharyngeal was placed and then Melissa started using the bag valve mask at 100%. Lorrie monitored her pulse and kept her neck in the neutral position. We both were crying and begging her to breathe. She looked like a rag doll, smelled like smoke, but yet so small and innocent. We were talking to her continuously. At 04:07 the first ambulance was departing the scene and heading to Loris Hospital while the second ambulance was on route to the scene for the second child, a seventeen-month-old boy.

The second child was found lying in his crib by fireman Jeff Fowler. When the infant was being brought down the ladder to the second ambulance crew, he looked like a mannequin, not a real baby. But, up close the sight of this infant was horrifying. The baby was in full cardiac arrest and he had such severe burns to his small body. Gary Watts jumped under the wheel of 2107 and drove while the crew, Ronnie and Sondra Watts, started CPR on the infant. At 04:14, both children were out of the burning house and on their way to the hospital without the mother who stayed behind.

The first ambulance arrived at the hospital at 04:13, only six minutes from leaving the burning home. The little girl was in critical care, but now she was alive with a pulse and breathing. When the second ambulance arrived in seven minutes, at 04:21, with little hope for the small infant boy who was still in cardiac arrest. At 04:48, the mother, grandmother, and boyfriend arrived at the ER. (So, that's where Hinson came up with the 48 minutes– accusing the rescue workers of the 48 minutes it took HER to get to the hospital.)

Lorrie had given the mother her coat at the scene of the house fire because it was a cool night and had gone into the triage room where they were to give her a blanket and to get her coat back. At 04:51 the little infant boy was pronounced dead by the ER Doctor and his sister laid in the next room fighting to breath because her carbon monoxide level was toxic. She was placed on a ventilator and was later moved to the Children's Pediatric Unit at Charleston's Medical University. She stayed in the hospital for six days and when she woke up, she had no problems, but plenty of questions. When she was told about her brother dying, she was told he was in heaven playing with the angels.

As for the little seventeen-month-old infant boy, the ambulance crew, Gary, Lorrie, and Melissa transported the infant to the Columbus County Morgue to be sent to Chapel Hill for an autopsy. That small infant hardly made an indention (indentation) in that big old stretcher.

The autopsy came back – cause of death was smoke inhalation. This call touched our hearts and lives and everyone that was involved in this call experienced a lot of emotions. This call only took three hours and twelve minutes, but it has lifetime scars. The entire Tabor City Rescue Squad went through a Stress Relief class on 10-21-96 to help cope or even understand, ask questions about this call and the ending.

On December 15, 1996, the crew members had the opportunity to meet the big brown-eyed little girl who they helped almost two months ago. Day after day of sick calls, wrecks, fires, and some tragedies, we volunteers, get our rewards by getting the rare opportunity of meeting our survivals.

Tabor City Rescue Squad

Coleman interviewed Emergency Rescue workers Lorrie Lancaster, Melissa Sykes, and Gary Sykes, who confirmed that when the first ambulance arrived, Terri Hinson was standing outside holding a cordless phone and cigarette case, wearing jeans, tennis shoes, glasses, and a short sleeve shirt. She came over to the ambulance and said, "You made me leave my babies." When Gary Sykes asked where the children were, Terri Hinson pointed to a window in the front of the house facing Wall Street which later turned out to be her own bedroom. Lorrie Lancaster observed that Hinson's hair was singed, but only on the ends. (Singed deliberately with the same hair curler used earlier that evening on her mother's hair?) Lorrie Lancaster loaned Terri Hinson a jacket, who walked around the ambulance to make more phone calls. Melissa heard the mother tell someone on the phone, "My babies are burned," which she should have had no way of knowing because the firemen were still in the house searching for Brittany and Josh.

Terri Hinson walked down the road toward the neighbors' rear driveway. She was about 20 yards away talking on the phone when Brittan y was brought out of the house and placed in the ambulance. She did not come toward the ambulance, nor did she request to ride with her daughter to the hospital.

All three rescue workers felt Terri Hinson was "faking" her emotions, that Terri Hinson had not acted like anyone else they had observed who had been through similar tragedies.

Coleman interviewed Michael Kent Jones, a partner in Wall Street Investment Company, and co-owner of the 101 Wall Street rental property along with Attorney Richard

160

Wright. Mr. Jones reported that he had received no complaints from the tenants (Rodney Strickland and Terri Hinson) as to a leaking roof or electrical problems. He had no knowledge of smoke detectors having been installed. in the house. "The man hired to fix faucets two months before the fire was an electrician and could have made changes in the light fixtures."

On October 25, 1996, or five days after the fatal fire, Lt. Michael Glenn, of the Tabor City Police received the following note accompanying a typed letter from Bryan Tripp, Terri Hinson's first husband, and father of Ashley, Bradley, and Timmie, who had been adopted.

To: LT. MICHAEL GLENN

Dear Lt. Glenn,

I hope you find this information helpful.
On Feb. 8, '82, I first met Terri L. Hinson. She was 17 and I was 23. We lived across the street from each other in Florence, SC. When we first started dating, her mom, Bernice Prince, told me she (Terri) had to be in by 10:30 pm. I thought she was one of those strict mothers and because she (Terri) was under 18.

I didn't find out until years later, the reason she had to be in so early was because she was on probation for B&E.

One weekend, we went to Charlotte to meet another family member. On the way, Terri told me about her troubled childhood. She told me about smoking pot and about her recent abortion. I could tell it troubled her to talk about these things.

When we arrived at her oldest sister's (Ann's) house, the first thing I saw in the house was on the coffee table. It was a big wooden bowl of pot.

It made me a little nervous, but I try not to judge

161

people and I knew we would not see them often.

After a few months of dating, we often talked about her troubled past. Terri said she didn't get to see her natural father and that her step-father, Earl, paid her little attention.

She mentioned often about her brother Ricky, who she claimed, raped her when she was five or six years old. But, she would also say she wasn't sure it happened, or if it did happen -- she blocked it from her memory.

On Terri's 18th birthday, she didn't have to be in so early. We began to see more of each other. She seemed obsessed with a baby her mom lost after she (Terri) was born. The baby girl would have been 1-2 years younger than Terri. The baby was born alive and suddenly died and was buried before Bernice ever left the hospital.

Terri always wanted to place a grave marker so the baby wouldn't be forgotten.

We talked a lot about her past behavior as she grew up and the little bits of trouble she got into, like shoplifting cigarettes and stuff like that.

I simply blew it off as a young girl trying to get attention.

Her step-father had a drinking problem. Bernice told me she would have to hold money back from Earl so she could buy stuff for her kids because Earl spent more on his kids than hers. This too, troubled Terri.

We were married on August 15, '82 at Timrod (?) Park in Florence, SC. My job didn't pay enough, so I decided to join the military.

In the meantime, we lived with my sister, Teresa, who was going through a divorce. We helped her with the kids while she worked, in exchange for a place to stay. It helped out both of us financially.

On Dec. 27, '82, I left for Lackland AFB for basic training. While there, I received letters from my mother and calls about Terri writing bad checks, going to jail, and my family bailing her out.

It really made it hard for me being 2,000 miles away and getting conflicting stories from my family and Terri.

During basic training, Terri's natural father Harry died. I was almost through with training and could not come home for the funeral.

After basic, I was allowed to come home for a week to find out what was going on for myself.

My father showed me all the stuff about the checks, jail, and the things they did to get her out of trouble.

It cost over $900.00 to straighten out the mess she'd caused. I gave Terri the benefit of the doubt and defended her to my family as simply being inexperienced in handling our finances.

I had planned to take her with me to Tech School in Illinois, but my parents wanted her to stay, find a job, and start paying them back.

Terri was not happy with this plan, but I asked her to do this to help smooth things over with my family.

My parents told Terri they would help her learn how to budget the money, but she would have to cooperate.

During the next few weeks at Tech School, Terri would call and tell me my parents were watching her every move and she felt like a prisoner. So, when I got paid, I wired her the money to come and join me at Tech School.

In the middle of the night, she left without telling anyone she was leaving.

I felt this (moving) would eliminate her stress and take the stress off my parents.

When I graduated from training, my first duty assignment was in Tampa, Florida. During this time, we were getting along great.

On the way to Tampa, we stopped in Nashville, Tenn. We were sightseeing and having fun. When we returned to the motel, she began having cramps on her side. Terri took some medicine and the pain eased.

We were at the Grand Ole Opry and she began having harder pains. I took her to a hospital and she had a cyst burst on one of her ovaries.

Two days later, we continued on to Tampa.

Once at MacDill AFB, we found a place to live. Three days after we got there, my mother died and we left Tampa as soon as we could get a flight out.

When we arrived in Columbia, my brother Charlie and my brother-in-law Chandler picked us up. On the way to Florence, Terri needed a nature break. While stopped, Charlie warned me not to take Terri into Dad's house.

My feelings were hurt and I was confused, but I blew it off as maybe it was just his emotions talking.

When we arrived at my Dad's house, Terri and I went in and as soon as my father saw my wife, he took her by the arm and lead her to the door.

I was upset and of course, Terri was upset. Terri ran across the street to her mom's and I followed.

I asked her why she was not allowed in the house. She said she didn't know why.

I went back to my Dad's home and he took me to his bedroom and told me Terri was not good to, or for, me, and if I stayed with her, nothing but trouble would be in my life.

I was really confused. Here it was my mom was dead and my father was hitting me with this stuff. My father said he had proof Terri was unfaithful to me while I was in Basic.

I gave Terri the benefit of the doubt again,

After my mother's funeral, we all sat down and Terri had the chance to defend herself. About 15 minutes into the kangaroo court, she left.

She never to this day denied any of the stuff they had against her. But, I forgave her if it did happen.

Later, we found out we were going to have our first child and my dad remarried.

Feb. 15, '84, Bradley was born. He was almost a month early, but he was healthy. He did have to stay a week longer than Terri and that bothered her somewhat.

During this time, Terri's step-father developed cancer and too, was dying.

I received a transfer to Shaw AFB in Sumter, SC to help her mom with Earl.

We were struggling, but surviving with the new baby.

Earl died and we found out again we were going to have a baby.

To help us out, we moved in with her mom.

At six months, Terri lost the baby and she blamed it on God and his way of punishing her for the abortion she had. The doctors said it was just one of those things they couldn't explain.

It helped being close to my Dad again.

Bernice spoiled Bradley like any grandparent would.

During Bernice's marriage to Terri's father, Harry was very abusive to Bernice. She often had flashbacks to the beatings she received.

She and I often argued and on several occasions, she tried to beat me with a belt. I tried not to fight her back and decided it was time for us to leave. We moved back to Sumter and later moved into Base Housing.

In 1987, we were going to have another baby. Terri started having problems early, so the doctors placed a stitch in her cervix to help support the weight of carrying a baby. It worked until Dec. 26, '87. When Ashley was born. She was two months early and stayed in the neo-natal unit until we brought her home in early Feb. '88.

Also, in Feb. '88, Terri's lung collapsed and she was sent to Ft. Gordon for surgery. This was only five weeks after Ashley was born.

While at Ft. Gordon, they did another pregnancy test. We both laugh on that one because we only had sex once and we just had a baby.

Well, again she was pregnant. Terri was ordered to have complete bed rest and they put the stitch in again.

Bernice came over to help me with Bradley and Ashley, who was on a heart monitor because of her prematurity, so Terri never got to bond with Ashley like a mother should bond with her baby.

I believe Terri resented the fact that her mom was taking care of Ashley.

In November, prior to Ashley being born, my father died. Before his death, he tried to make peace with Terri.

Nov. 1, '88, Timothy was born. Terri carried him to term with no problems. Terri bonded with Timmy immediately. Bernice, for some reason, seemed to resent Timmy because she'd say Timmy looked and acted like the Hinsons, Terri's natural father.

Terri did resent those statements her mother was making.

When Timmy was older, and being a typical little boy, Bernice would spank him hard enough she left marks on his butt and when I demanded she stop, she would start trying to swing at me.

Bernice would yank Timmy up by his arms. Bernice never spanked Bradley or Ashley like that.

Terri saw her mom do this to Timmy often. Terri did deeply resent her mom for treating Timmy different than the other two.

Bernice was constantly meddling in our business. If I didn't do exactly what her mom wanted me to do, she'd tell Terri I was no good.

Terri was getting restless with our marriage. She often stated she didn't know what she wanted anymore. Terri would call me at work and say the kids were driving her crazy.

They were simply being kids. I know it was stressful,

but that's what happens when you become parents.

Terri never finished any job or projects she started. There was always some excuse to quit.

Our marriage was failing and I was trying to hold on for the kid's sake.

Terri was not a bad mom when we were married. At times, she became lazy with being a mother. She never harmed the kids. She was confused about what she wanted out of life.

I always told her you can't live life in the past.

I suggested we have an open marriage. For the next two weeks, we were like newlyweds again.

Then, one day she asked me if I had been seeing anyone. I said, "No," because I would feel guilty, but someone had to make the first move.

Well, I had to eat my words, because the next day, she slept with my supervisor at work.
From that point on, the marriage was a marriage of convenience.

I was discharged from the military because of downsizing.

So, we had nowhere to go except to Bernice's, who now lived in Fair Bluff, NC.

Bernice always blamed me for Terri's problems.

Bernice and Terri demanded I stay home and collect unemployment checks until Terri could go to school and find herself a job. It was fine with me because I liked taking care of the kids. I did this for about a month.

The job service called and said they found me a job and if I didn't accept it, my checks would stop. I had gone to a job fair in Columbia, SC and the same day was offered a job as assistant manager to a major convenience store chain. I took that job because there was a better chance for advancement faster. The starting pay was not great, but I knew I couldn't start at the top.

Bernice was so mad I took the job. Terri was not happy either.

I was working on the 10th day and got a phone call that Terri's other lung had collapsed. Bernice refused to help me watch the kids so I could continue to work and try to comfort my ailing wife in the hospital. So, I was forced to quit and stay home to take care of the kids. And, because it was not the employer's fault, I could not resume unemployment benefits.

Now there was no income coming in, so Welfare saved my kids from starving. I was able to receive Food Stamps, Medicare for the kids, and some foundation paid the hospital bills.

I had applied to work at the local prison. They were expanding. And every week or so, I'd get a letter that construction was being delayed and my hire date kept changing.

Also, everyday bill collectors were calling wanting payments. So, I had no choice but to find something to hold us over, so I got a job at another store working third shift. I was in the Reserves and now with this little job and the little money I was making, it was getting a little less stressful, money-wise.

As soon as I would get home around 7 am, Terri would leave, telling me she was going to help her mom at the restaurant, where Bernice worked (as a waitress). Sometimes Bradley would be ready for school, so I'd take him, get Ashley and Timmy to day-care, get back to the house at 8:30 am, get three or four hours of sleep, go and get Ashley and Timmy from day-care, wait for Bradley to get home, and watch them until Terri returned.

Later, I would find out that Bernice had been covering for Terri to sneak off with her boyfriend.

While I was working at the store, Terri's brother, Ricky, was killed in a car crash. This was the brother she

168

claimed had raped her. The old feeling returned and for some reason, she felt guilty about his death and blamed herself for him dying.

On Sept. 3, '91, I finally was hired to work at the prison. The month before, all our household goods were sold because I couldn't afford to pay the storage costs. The bin was in Terri's name so they sent her a check for over $1,000.00. She never gave me a penny, but wasted it on nothing.

We were still sleeping together and having sex, but we were still passing each other every day.

My first few days at work was prison orientation. On the next Friday, I was to have my first exposure to the inmates. I had to be in at 2:00 pm and I needed to leave the house by 1:00 pm to get to work on time. After work, I was leaving for weekend Reserve drill at Charleston, SC.

Bernice came home as I was putting my suitcase in the car. She asked where I was going and I told her.

I put Ashley and Timmy down for their naps. I was in my uniform and was waiting for Terri to come home so I could leave for work.

Bernice said she didn't know where Terri was. Terri knew what time I needed to leave.

Bernice demanded I rake the yard before I left. I told her I'd rake it on Monday because I was off. Bernice said if I didn't rake the yard, I would not have a place to live on Sunday when I returned from duty. Then Bernice began to yell at me because we had been living with her and not paying her any money to do so. She began to tell me how sorry I was, that I was a bad husband and a sorry father. Bernice was out of control.

I finally had to leave because Terri never showed up. Bernice again threatened to throw me out.

On Sunday morning, I called to talk to Terri. She said my clothes were on the front porch. Knowing how these two

169

women operated, I went to my sister's house and had her type a letter to give them stating I was being forced out against my will and I was not leaving my kids because I wanted to.

When I arrived at Bernice's home I was asked to give them my keys and not allowed to enter the house. Terri had a hand-written Separation Agreement in her hand. So, to keep from causing a scene in front of my kids, I got my clothes and left.

I had no money or anywhere to go, but somehow, I managed to survive.

Terri and I had talked about this prior to them throwing me out. We agreed to let me get two full months of paychecks so I could find a place to live and so I could see the kids on visitation days. But, I was forced to live in a rat and roach-infested trailer, not fit for dogs to live in.

A friend of mine worked for DSS and said the State would never let the kids stay with me as long as I lived in that trailer. But, I wanted to see my children and out of desperation, allowed them to see me and stay with me. I had no money to have the heat cut on.

Terri and her mom found out where I lived and constantly harassed me. They would come over day and night. I'd have to park my car in my landlord's barn to stop them from stopping by. They would always bring the kids knowing I would never slam the door on my children and I never did. When the door was open, Terri and her mom would come barreling in fussing and cussing me about one thing or another. The kids would always hear the arguing.

I went to training for my prison job right away.

One weekend I was home and Terri came up with the kids alone. She gave me this song and dance about Bradley needing medical care and the doctors wouldn't accept my insurance. I wrote her a post-dated check for $400.

After I got to thinking about it, it didn't sound quite right. So, I tried to stop payment on the check. She beat me to the bank and the $400 check cost me $800, because of the bad checks I had written not knowing the stop payment didn't stop payment.

Bernice got in touch with me one day and told me she had thrown Terri out because Terri made several attempts to leave the kids alone. They were only 7, 4, and 3 years old. Bernice also filed charges at DSS for Protective Custody against Terri. Bernice told me she had given Terri money to go to school and to pay her bills and Terri and her boyfriend went to the beach and spent it all. Bernice also told me she realized our marital problems weren't all my fault. Bernice asked me if Terri was on drugs again. I never saw Terri take any drugs, but she did fit the ads about someone who was on drugs.

I tried my best to work and help Bernice with the kids. There was a conflict once and I couldn't watch the kids one night. I asked Bernice if Terri could watch them just that night. She said she did not want her daughter around the kids because they would not be safe.

DSS ruled there wasn't enough evidence for protective custody.

One time, Terri and her boyfriend threatened to take the kids to Ohio.

One of the solutions was to place the kids in foster care until it could be determined who was more fit to take custody.

Bernice said she would take care of them so it would not disrupt their lives any more than it already had. I agreed.

Terri called me at work and told me her mom had found families to adopt the children. At first, I was totally against this idea. I didn't want to give my kids away. But after much thought and prayer, I decided it would be best for the kids to get in a stable home and have a greater chance at life than what I could give them. Besides, I had no funds to fight them. Plus, Terri would be out of their lives, but her mom still got to be their grandmother.

Terri's mom convinced her to sign the papers for adoption. For me, it was the hardest thing I ever had to do. But, I did it because I loved my kids so deeply.

Ashley and Timmy went first, leaving only Bradley. Terri changed her mind about Bradley's adoption. Both Bernice and I agreed it was BECAUSE Terri had just had another baby (Brittany) by her boyfriend, and she wanted a built-in babysitter.

Bernice again convinced Terri to sign the papers.

In April '93, I filed for a divorce and was granted an absolute divorce.

I didn't hear from Terri until April '94, when I had to sign some paper that I was not the father of the child she had while we were legally separated. She knew the child was not mine. (1) I was not with her when the baby was conceived. (2) I could prove I was living in Ellerbee, NC, and (3) I had had a vasectomy just after we found out she was pregnant with Timmy in 1988.

This summary is not intended by myself, Bryan L. Tripp, to be hateful, spiteful, or in any way intended to get even for what Terri's mother had done to me while we were married and separated. It is the truth as I remember it and as it was told to me by Terri L. Hinson and Bernice B. Prince.

And, these memories were only the highlights. There were other stuff that was left out.

If I can be of any further assistance, please don't hesitate to call.

Sincerely,

Bryan L Tripp

To whom it may concern:

The purpose of this letter is to let it be known, and made clear, that I, Bryan L. Tripp, am being forced out of my present residence, leaving behind my wife and children, against my will.

My mother-in-law, Bernice Prince, has threatened, on more than one occasion, to throw me out of her house, where I have resided for 9 months with my family, leaving me with nowhere to live. I have left the date on this letter open and I will fill it in when the incident occurs.

This letter was typed the weekend of 9-7-91, while I was serving my weekend Reserve duty in Charleston. I was told by Ms. Prince that I may find my personal belongings in the yard upon my return Sunday evening. Should this happen, it will be done totally against my wishes to leave my family.

Bryan L. Tripp

     Coleman interviewed Bryan Tripp, who recalled he met Terri Hinson in 1982, when the Hinson's moved across the street in Florence, SC. "I was 22. Terri was 17. Our parents arranged a blind date. "Terri had to be in by 10:00. I thought it was because her mother was strict. After we got married, I found out Terri had to be home early because Terri was on probation. She'd already had an abortion. She was starved for affection. Her step-father never paid her any attention. He was a salesman and had to travel a lot. He was an alcoholic – drink a case or a fifth every night. The first weekend we dated, we went to visit Terri's sister Anne in Charlotte. I walk in the door and there's a big wooden bowl in the middle of the room filled with pot. We get ready to go visit Terri's other sister, Linda, and as they get in my car, Anne's boyfriend stuffs a .357 Magnum in his pocket.

     We dated for a while. She would break up. After 6 months, we got married, but her mother said I couldn't marry her daughter unless I joined the military. We married in

August. I joined the Air Force in December. Terri began partying. My family said she was running around. She only wrote to me twice during my six weeks in Basics.

Terry's real father died. He used to shoot spiders.

Terry claimed that when she was 5, her brother Ricky either raped her or she dreamed he did. Ricky was hot. The day before he was killed, he was in court for DUI's. He and his father were real close. Terri said she remembered her father beat her mother.

Terri went to jail for writing $900 worth of bad checks. My parents got her out. Later, she sold Avon to my family and kept the money. My dad would say Terri was making it difficult while I was in basics. She wasn't paying the bills.

After basics, I took a week off. My parents said we needed to talk. They told me about the bad checks. I refused to believe them. I got my first paycheck for Basics and called home. Terri said, "Your family is driving me crazy! Can I come with you to the Air Force Base in Illinois?"

Everything went great for a month. We left April 20, 1983, to the Air Force Base in Tampa. On the way, we stopped in Nashville. Terri started complaining of pains. She had a ruptured cyst on her ovary.

I got a call my mother had died. My sister said don't bring her (Terri) home for the funeral. On the way from the airport, my brother told me not to bring Terri to my father's house. We went into the house. When my father saw Terri, he ushered her out of the house. She's been running around with men who worked with my Dad. My sister said Terri was hitting on her friend's husband. My family had pictures of men Terri had been with and accused Terri of writing bad checks.

Terri walked out, saying, "I don't have to put up with this shit!"

About six months later, I called my Dad and said Terri

was pregnant. I told my family I had forgiven Terri and expected them to do the same.

We went home for three days leave and to attend my father's wedding.

February, 1984, Bradley was born. My father came to Tampa to celebrate the birth of his first grandchild.

Justice for Baby Josh

Earl, Terri's step-father had cancer. I got transferred closer to home. Things were going ok. While we were in Fair Bluff, Terri insisted we go to the cemetery. She said she had a sister who died of mysterious causes. (killed by Harry Hinson in 1965 or 1966?), she was known as "Baby Girl Hinson."

Bernice (Terri's mother) said she married Harry Hinson (20 years older) to get out of her house.

Bernice loved Bradley to death, but she said Timmy had the Hinson look and that made her mad. She would hit Timmy hard. She'd grab him by the arm and beat him til he had hand prints on his buttocks leaving marks. Terri said nothing to stop her.

Terri's step-father Earl died in 1984-5.

Terri had a miscarriage at six months, between Bradley and Ashley. We moved in with Bernice. Terri looked for work. One day Bernice came after me with a belt and started hitting me with it. She was hot or cold. She'd get pissed off for little things.

Terri got depressed after the still-born. Got pregnant with Ashley. Had complications. "Weak womb." A lot of times sex was like sleeping with a dead person.

A lot of times I came home from work and they wouldn't even give supper a thought. She acted like something was missing in her life. She took a job at Captain D's. We were paying more to the babysitter than Terri was making. She couldn't get along with the manager, so she quit. after two weeks. She worked two days, twisted her ankle, stayed home, so they fired her. Next, she worked at Pizza Hut for a week and quit. She never followed through with anything she started. She started volunteer work with the Red Cross and became head volunteer in six weeks. We had three children in day-care. We started having conflicts. Terri quit and went back to staying at home.

I got two pounds overweight, so the Air Force

176

assigned me to a desk job. Terri would come by. The
marriage was dead. We were always arguing. Terri was
complaining all the time that she couldn't go to school. She
was blaming me for having to stay home with the kids.
Bernice was feeding the fire.

Terri was having an affair with my supervisor for
about a year. Bernice blamed me for her daughter's affair. We
moved to Bernice's in Fair Bluff, North Carolina. Bernice
and Terri told me to stay home with the kids and let Terri go
to school to become a phlebotomist. She'd leave me with the
kids and never go to school.

I took a job in Florence as assistant store manager.
Ten days into the job, Terri's lung collapsed. She was
hospitalized for 3-4 days. I lost my job because Bernice
wouldn't watch the kids. Bernice was a waitress. She got
pissed off because I ironed clothes. I took a third-shift job.
When I'd get home, in the morning, Terri would leave, but
wouldn't tell me where. Bernice claimed Terri was helping at
the restaurant, but she was with her boyfriend. His name was
Phillip something.

I got a job as a prison guard. I was supposed to be at
work orientation. I called Terri to come home so I could get
to work. Bernice came home.

I was ready to go to weekend Air Force Reserves drill
that weekend. Terri's sister Linda was coming to visit.
Bernice told me, "You got to rake the yard." She went crazy.
"If you leave this house, you won't have a place to live when
you get back." I called Terri. She told me Bernice had put all
my stuff out in the yard. I had my sister type a letter saying I
was being forced out. Terri demanded my key and handed me
a handwritten Separation Agreement. I picked up my stuff
and slept in my car. I stayed with my pastor one night. Then
the prison sent me to school for four weeks.

Terri got mad because I wouldn't take the kids. I was
working every weekend. Terri and Bernice found out where I

was living. They would come to the house and begin telling me how to live my life. I'd have to hide my car to keep them from harassing me. I called the Magistrate, who told me to call her lawyer, but the Magistrate refused to file a Restraining Order for me, so I transferred to another prison unit.

One time, Bernice brought Ashley and Timmy to my house. "Take a good look at your daughter because this is the last time you'll ever see her." I didn't have any heat in my trailer anyway.

Terri had moved back with her mother. Bernice had given Terri some money to pay bills. Terri went to the beach with her boyfriend and spent all the money. Bernice threw Terri out of her house.

I'd drive to Fair Bluff and watch the kids while Bernice was waitressing.

I'd met someone and told Bernice. I couldn't watch the kids, so I'd get Terri to. Bernice said she didn't want Terri around the kids. Terri had been leaving the kids alone while she was running around. Bernice had come home and found the children alone in the house. Terri had gone. Bernice had even tried to get a Protective Custody Order against Terri.

Terri calls me at work. Bernice threatens to bring the children to the prison.

The State of North Carolina was getting ready to put my kids in foster care. I couldn't take them in the trailer because I didn't have any heat. I'd have to wait six months to a year to get custody.

Terri calls me through Prison Emergency. Her mother had contacted some females who wanted to adopt Ashley and Timmy. "Don't let that happen," she tells me.

I was voluntarily sending $200 a month to Bernice for child support. Bernice still refused to let me see my kids.

I was sent to attorney Sauls' office. Terri is crying. Terri signed the adoption papers for Ashley and Timmy.

Bernice went to keep Bradley. But, the church said they'd found a home for Bradley in Kentucky. Bernice still wouldn't let me talk to Bradley and said, "Your Daddy doesn't love you." I signed the papers.

Bernice called at my job for me to sign the final papers on Bradley's adoption. Terri, who had run off with her boyfriend to Charlotte for a month or two, moved back with Bernice. She and Bernice met me in Rockingham. Terri tells me, "I'm suing you. The Drs. said you gave me cancer." I said, "Sue me." Bernice had given us a nice microwave. She demanded it back.

Coleman's impression of Bryan Tripp was that Mr. Tripp was an essentially good and honest person, naive perhaps, but certainly wanting to believe the best in people. In other words, there was nothing in his character, background, or experience which prepared him for the treachery, sociopathy, and criminality of the Hinson clan. In a word, Terri and Bernice Hinson snuck up behind, hit him over the head with a 2x4, which sent him reeling and helpless through a nightmare which lasted 10 years.

Listening to Bryan Tripp recount his 10 years of living with Terri Hinson puts the reader inside Terri Hinson's head, as well as bearing witness to her callous indifference, open hostility, neglect and abandonment she showed her first three children.

Rather than being the victim of a tyrannical DSS, Terri Hinson seems to have abandoned her children to run off with a new boyfriend, and when unable to force their father -- her husband, to take the three children off her hands, she voluntarily signed adoption papers on each of her three children.

Terri Hinson had not only lied to the police as to the circumstances of her having "already lost" her three children, but she tried to cover-up past acts of getting rid of her children when they stood in the way of her relationships with boyfriends.

Undated letter written sometime in February, 1992, by Bernice Prince (Terri's mother) to DSS

Just before Thanksgiving Terri tried to commit suicide by taking Quinine & different pills that were here. She was never here for the children. She received checks & support for children & never spent one penny on children or for children. I bought all their clothes, food, & medicine until 1-14-92. Jan 2nd Terri took Bradley to Dr. Melser for possibly a very bad kidney infection. The same day she got a check for $297.00 (AFDC). Also, a Medicaid card & then with both, she didn't get Bradley's medicine as important as it is. On Mon. Jan. 13, I went to the doctor's office & had him recall the prescription & went up & bought it for him.

Terri has been going with Phil Williams since the 1st of Sept before she and Bryan separated. On one occasion, I come home & found her standing naked in my home where she and Phil had just crawled out of bed.

I have cared for Bradley, Ashley, and Timmie for the past 4 months or more. No matter how many hours I worked Terri would walk out & leave me with the children never being anything for them. She & Phil took about $1,800 of my money I had for bills & completely blew it on motels & riding up & down the road.

I have done my best to create a loving home for the children. I would give my right arm if I could quit work & stay home & care for them. Terri & Phil, on or about Nov. 5, was going to take Bradley out of school, take Timmie & Ashley & just take off, not once thinking of the welfare of the children & go to Ohio. Neither has a job, no money, no nothing. Terri is going to give excuses of not having a car to go to work. But, I let her drive my car. I told her just a week & half ago that if she got a job she could still use my car.

Justice for Baby Josh

Ask anyone anywhere from here to Valdesta, what kind of a mom I have been & what kind of a Mema (grandma) I've been. Last Sunday a week ago, I wanted to go see my brother that was hurt. She told me she would leave the children alone so I kept them. I have tried everything I know to help Terri. I tried sending her back to school. She has done nothing. I am her mother & I honestly don't believe she will ever be able to provide & take care of the children financially, mentally, or physical. If I thought different I would be in 100% agreement with her having them. I love these children & pray God will watch over them & take care of them.

Sincerely Bernice B. Prince

On March 25, 1992, the Columbus County Department of Social Services found charges of "neglect" against Terri L Tripp "to be true. We will be providing Protective Services to the children."

On June 13, 1995, the Columbus County Department of Social Services investigated complaints that Terri Hinson was leaving her two-month-old son, Josh Hinson alone in the car while she was attending classes at Southeastern Community College, taking him where there would be large numbers of people, having him around people who smoke, and taking him out of the house, while he is on a Heart Monitor. The Social Services investigator stated the "maltreatment" has been going on for 3-4 days after Josh was born. Josh was described as being neglected in that he "does not receive proper care, supervision, or discipline," and because he is considered a "special needs" child, a response to the allegations of neglect must receive a response within 24 hours.

According to the report, the onetime Social Services investigated the complaint that Terri Hinson was leaving infant Josh alone in the car while she attended classes, a

181

student said she had been asked to watch Josh. However, had Columbus County Social Services done more than this one time superficial investigation, they would have confirmed that (1) Josh's mother was a habitual smoker, (2) that having her infant son on a Heart Monitor and having been instructed by Josh's doctor not to smoke around Josh, she had willfully failed to reduce her smoking, according to her two closest friends, Betty Gore, and Dana Hammond. (3) Similarly, in violation of the doctor's orders, Terri Hinson took Josh out while he was wearing his heart monitor, took him to class, brought him on campus around large numbers of people, and in fact, Coleman recalls she brought Josh into the classroom full of students on at least three occasions, and (4) by thus putting Josh in harm's way, Terri Hinson should have been found guilty of gross neglect, and placed under supervision.

Terri Hinson was a dangerous parent and had been for years. Had DSS taken the time to read the signs, Josh's life could have been saved.

On August 21, 1998, Coleman interviewed Ernestine McQueen, who lives across the street from Bernice Hinson, and has lived in the neighborhood since she was six years old. Mrs. McQueen said, "I introduced Bernice to Earl," (Bernice's second husband and Terri's step-father.)

"I remember seeing Bernice trailing kids down the street. Bernice had Willis (her first husband) run out of the state. He came to my door one night with blood all over his face from where Bernice had hit him.

Bernice had indicted her son Ricky for raping one of his sisters (Terri?). Bernice was always bad-mouthing Willis and turning the kids against their father. Bernice got hell-fire in her.

When my mother had a stroke, Bernice dug up the flowers that had been given my mother over the years.

Earl took Bernice on cruises and bought three houses. He worked on the road. Terri would steal things from his truck. Terri broke into the church parsonage and wrote out a check to the church. She got a job at a convenience store in Wilmington, only to get caught stealing.

Bernice had boyfriends. She was a waitress and stole clothes from the factory.

Terri created problems for the marriage. Bernice lied for Terri.

Earl left his Will in his Post Office box. Bernice raised hell about the Will to have everything put in her name. He agreed. They moved to Florence into a nice home.

Terri would lie all the time. So, would her mother.

Bernice was going to leave Earl as he was going into surgery for lung cancer. He made out a new Will. Bernice didn't know about the second Will. Bernice got money for the three houses, some cash, plus life insurance. Bernice refused to give anything to Earl's children they had wanted. After the Will was read, Bernice and Terri got into the car and left.

I have never seen love in the Hinson house. Bernice said she wished baby Josh would have been born dead. Bernice said to me that Terri thought the boyfriend loved her and Terri was going to give Josh up for adoption. When Josh's grandmother said, she would take Josh; however, Terri decided to keep him.

Bernice told everybody after Earl's death that she had no money. She probably got $75, 000 to $100,000. She bought that house in Fair Bluff.

The first time I saw the children (Bradley, Ashley, and Timmy) after Terri moved here, I saw children playing in the yard. The dog started to cross the highway with the children following. I raced into the street to save the children. No adults were around. I knocked on Bernice's door. She told me she thought the screen door had been locked.

Brittany is also starved for attention. She goes in and out of the fence. Terri is wrapped up in Terri. I'd call Bernice at her restaurant to tell her that the children were playing on the edge of the highway. Bradley would beg people to take him home with them. He'd ask neighbors not to make him go home. I've seen Bradley playing outside without shoes or socks while Terri's in the house with her boyfriend.

Not long after Earl's death, Bernice took Earl's old Will to Probate, not knowing about the new Will.

A cook in the restaurant saw Bernice slap Bradley in the face so hard – She's evil.

Bernice went to California to see her oldest son. While she was gone, Terri's carrying on with her boyfriend. After Bernice came home, Terri took off to Charlotte with her boyfriend and left the children with Bernice.

I've seen Brittany riding her bike on the highway and cars had to stop to keep from hitting her.

I've never seen Terri holding or loving on her children. One time, I heard Brittany start screaming, "She"s (her mother) bad! Get away from that woman – she's been to my Me-Ma!"

The morning after the fire, Bernice came over to tell me, "You need to tell them Terri lived here with me and she's a good mother."

Bernice told me soon after the fire that while she was there (at Terri's) the evening of the fire, having Terri fix her hair that the (hair) blower sparked. Bernice said, "That could start the fire." Bernice told me that Terri had slept downstairs in case the house caught fire. Josh's door was closed so tight, she couldn't get the door open. She (Terri) heard Brittany calling. Terri couldn't get to Brittany because of smoke.

Bernice found Terri's new husband announced in the paper. Terri came between us (Bernice?) We had to part company.

Terri was always sick – not able to work.

Linda, (Terri's sister) told her best friend that Terri "did it." Bernice brow-beats them to death.

I've never known Terri to have had a full-time job

since the convenience store job.

In the "Quickly-Two" convenience store in Whiteville, someone had placed a jar asking for donations for Josh and Brittany. The person (Rodney?) who picked up the jar went around the corner and bought beer with the money.

Bernice was calling everyone after the fire saying that, "We are going to sue the people who own the house.

Terri was always bossing her husband telling them what to do. Now that she's no longer on house arrest, Terri never goes to the cemetery (to visit Josh's grave).

Bernice's brother told Bernice to stop putting all that "God stuff" in Brittany's head.

Bernice told me that the Judge ordered that Terri could see children (Bradley, Ashley, and Timmy) when she wanted and Bernice could put children where she wanted. Terri said, "Good, now I don't have to get up with them."

Bernice said she got swindled out of $50,000. He would invest her $50,000. It was in the paper. Then she claimed it was Harry Lee's money.

Bernice got Federal funds to fix up the house after collecting Earl's money.

Charles, around 40, "A little bit off," a homosexual who has boyfriends. Bradley spent a lot of time over there and begged to live with Charles.

Another neighbor, Adelle, has seen Bernice and Terri slap the children, yelling and hollering at them.

Terri wrote an article about a teacher slapping Bradley on his hand – a Letter to the Editor when Bradley was in the second grade.

This (the fire) is all about attention and to get money out of them (the owners of the burned house) Rodney and Terri were going to be rich.

Rodney stayed with his aunt Geneva the night of the fire. His son is a deputy sheriff. Terri called her mother first to tell her the house is on fire. Bernice drove to Geneva's house to pick up Rodney. (How did Bernice know where Rodney was that night? Why didn't Rodney stay at his mother's?)

"I never saw any grief or sadness – only threats to sue."

Ernestine McQueen's corroborates Terri Hinson's pattern of physical and emotional abuse, gross neglect, and abandonment of her children, her history of lying, stealing, promiscuity, and the criminal extent to which she will go to get money.

On August 25, 1998, Coleman interviewed Attorney Sauls, the attorney who handled the adoption of two of Terri Hinson's children, adoptions she claimed had been done behind her back while she was in Charlotte with her boyfriend, Phillip Gene Williams, Brittany's father.

Justice for Baby Josh

Attorney Sauls stated, "The mother, (Terri Hinson) played an active part in the adoption of all three of her children. Terri wasn't capable of caring for children. She left all three with their grandmother (Bernice) who had to do something because she couldn't take care of them either. No one was pushing for adoption. It was more a matter of their mother defaulting on motherhood, and grandmother having no choice."

Terri Hinson signed the adoption papers for Ashley Tripp and Timothy Tripp on March 2, 1992, listing her address as 9128 Detroiter Rd., Huntersville, NC 28078, but signed the papers in the Columbus County Clerk of Court's office in Whiteville, NC, thereby contradicting her claim that the adoption had taken place while she was in Charlotte, that her mother had arranged the adoptions behind her back and without her knowledge or consent, and that she knew nothing about the adoption until she returned from being in Charlotte for several months.

Coleman located Phillip Gene Williams, Terri's boyfriend, while she was still married to Bryan Tripp, Mr. Williams, who would father Brittany, said he met Terri in 1991, at her cousin's house, Ann Ward.

"Terri was married to Tripp, but she made him (Tripp) leave. We had been dating. She filed for Separation from Tripp 9/17/91. Terri was living at home. We were now dating more heavily. She was leaving children more and more. I tried to tell her to take care of her kids. They were running around without underwear. Her mother was also hard on her. In January, 1992, Terry moved out to her cousin's house. I spent the night. She left her kids at her mother's. Terri's mother called DSS and begged Tripp to take the kids.

Terri and her cousin had a falling out, "snapping at kids" and may have slapped them. Her cousin Ann chased Terri out with a butcher knife. Terri knocked on my window at 5:00 am, saying she had walked all the way from Fair Bluff, 14 miles. I took her back to her mother's and left. Her mother rented a room above the restaurant/motel.

Two of Terri's kids were adopted before she went to Charlotte. She went to Charlotte first to get away from town talk. Her oldest boy (Bradley) stayed with the grandmother. Terri kept coming back from Charlotte. In March, I moved to Charlotte. Worked one week. She worked at a rabbit research place. She was sick all the time. I laid brick for one week.

She planned on marriage. Terri was already pregnant. I left. She came and got me to go back to Charlotte. Diane (?) moved in with us. December, 1992, Terri said she had cervical cancer and had to go home. I went to my mother's. Terri had Brittany, 9/92, three weeks premature. The hospital called DSS to come get the child because Terri wouldn't come see the child.

In April, 1993, we moved to Conway. Brittany was nasty because Terri was not taking care of her. Terri was riding up and down the road. I'd caught her in her car kissing another man in Charlotte. I couldn't catch her other times.

I lost my job. I was drinking. I did love her, but she drove me to drink. She went back to her mother's. I became disabled. She got me for child support, then terminated my parental rights. I got depressed and went into the hospital twice.

I didn't want anything to do with her. In August, 1994, my uncle was murdered.

I've had no communication with Terri since Court. She'd told me in 9/91, she couldn't get pregnant." (Four years later, Terri told Josh's father the same lie in order to trick him into getting her pregnant.)

Brittany Lola Williams was born September 10, 1992. Terri left the father's name blank on Brittany's Birth Certificate. By Order filed by Terri Hinson, Phillip Gene Williams consented to have his parental rights terminated, and by Order signed on the 24th of October, 1994, Brittany's name was changed from Brittany Lola Williams to Brittany Denise Hinson.

On September 10, 1998, Coleman took a statement from Betty Gore, also one of his psychology students, and Terri Hinson's self-described closest friend (before the fire).

Betty recalled first meeting Terri while they were both students at Southeastern Community College in 1995. At the time, Terri was living in the Tabor Villa Apartments. Terry was seven months pregnant (Josh).

She had not yet met Rodney Strickland. Terri said, "I want to meet that man." According to Terri, Brittany's father was crazy and had done bad things. She said she wanted to hurry up and have Josh so she could have a child by Rodney.

She and Rodney only dated four weeks. Rodney was already saying, "I'm not having any more damn children to have to pay child support for." Rodney confided to Betty, "Terri's trying to get pregnant to set me up."

Terry was company. He (Rodney) wasn't interested in sex. He couldn't afford any more children, but that didn't stop Terri from trying to get pregnant before and after Josh was born.

Rodney was at home, seeing Terri, and having problems with both of his sons. His oldest son wrecked a motorcycle, so Rodney would have to take his son back to Camp Lejeune. Terri got pissed because Rodney would be gone and not with her.

Terri would call every night to tell me what a bad wife Rodney had. Rodney and Terri started following her. Rodney's wife had an affair with a physician's assistant to make Rodney jealous. They saw him.

Terri said the physician's assistant was staying nights near the Sheriff's Department. He had a key. He and Terri were having sex. Terri told Rodney to leave his wife or she'll continue to have the affair.

He'd call when I was visiting Terri. He had written a prescription. Terri said, "I can get anything from him I want. All I have to do is call."

Terri said she sent Rodney to the doctor. Found out he's diabetic.

Terri asked me to adopt Josh and Brittany and gave me large pictures of both children.

When Rodney threatened me – anybody who testified against Terri – "I'll get them."

Terri bought a blue dress for TV saying, "I'm not going to be another Susan Smith. (Mother who drowned her two little boys because the rich man with whom she was having an affair didn't want anyone with kids).

Justice for Baby Josh

Terri said, "When the grandchild (Josh) is born, things are going to happen." Terri looked at me like she did at Brittany at the hospital – "You shouldn't be alive."

My boyfriend Larry had been with the Loris Fire Dept. Terri and I had to do papers for college. Terry asked Larry, "What's a 'flashover'?" She had gone to the library to get a book on fires.

I didn't have a typewriter, so Terri was typing my papers and Rodney was helping tutor three times a week. They were staying at Tabor Villa Apartments. One time she called, "Brittany is driving me crazy. If you'll get Brittany out of my hair, I'll do your papers."

Terri's always wears blue jeans and shirts. She said after her husband beat her, she needed to be ready to get out.

I frequently got on her, "This baby smells like spoiled milk." Her answer was to stick her kids with whoever would take them and then send them to bed as soon as possible.

Rodney spanked Brittany. He'd left a hand print. That caused lots of problems between them. Terri was really angry with Rodney. Terri said Brittany was causing a lot of problems. She asked me to adopt her kids, "so Rodney and I can make it." There was a lot of pressure between Terri and Rodney and money, and Rodney and divorce. If the landlord found out that Terri and Rodney were not married, they'd be put out.

Rodney's sons were in trouble. Rodney wanted his son Jeremy to move in, but he and Terry didn't get along. "It wouldn't work." Jeremy also refused. Rodney would go back to Jeremy and Terri would pitch a fit. We followed Rodney and Terri. The ex was trying to get Rodney back.

Terri would call and say, "He's fooling around. I'm not spending my weekends by myself while he's up there with his damn wife!" Terri hated that woman. Rodney stayed to get her back – make Terri jealous.

191

Justice for Baby Josh

The night of the fire, Terri called around 4:00 am. "Betty, this is Terry. The house caught fire. The children are hurt. I'm at the Loris Hospital.

We jump up and drive to the hospital. Terri, Rodney, and Bernice were there. Terri was crying a little bit. "Josh is dead," she said. I hugged her. It was more like she had lost an animal.

Bernice wasn't crying. She was at a pay phone. She slammed the receiver down. "Oh, my God! Oh, my God."

Five minutes after we arrived, Terri said, "Let's go outside and smoke a cigarette."

The doctor gave Terri a pill. Her hair was singed. a little bit – more like someone had bent over. It was singed from the top of the head down – not sides or back. More like she had stuck her head in the fire. I don't know.

I thought Rodney was dazed.

The nurse said we could see Brittany. Terri went in and came out and told me to go back home and get my pocketbook (for money to give to Terri) I said, "No." Terri had already written a permission letter for me at the hospital.

When they went back to the house to get Terri's pocketbook, they started taking out videos, briefcases, and clothes, walking right across the police crime scene tape. The police arrived while they were taking things out of the house. It was unusual getting videos, bread, food, clothing, Rodney's briefcases – taking stuff out by the arm loads. Bernice was acting like she expected Brittany to die – so cold-hearted.

We arrived in Charleston before lunch. They didn't get there until supper time --6:00 -6:30 pm.

I got to see Brittany. She was asleep. They thought she was going to make it. I was in Brittany's room when Terri, Rodney, and Bernice arrived. The nurse had been asking all afternoon, "Where's the girl's mother?"

Terri maybe spent five minutes with Brittany. They couldn't believe Brittany was still alive. Terri said, "Oh yes, she's a fighter."

They started questioning the nurse about where they could spend the night. She told them the Ronald McDonald House. Terri and her mother went to make a phone call. Terri asked me, "Will you go back and stay with Brittany. I need to make a phone call. "You're going to stay here tonight with Brittany."

I told Terri, "You need to be here."

Terri called – said babysitter was on the way to look after Brittany.

We got ready to leave. Terri had already left to have a cigarette. The Nurse got disgusted. "The mother needs to be here when Brittany comes around."

Larry and I left. Terri said she was leaving, too. She told the nurse she had a babysitter on the way. That was Sunday evening – the day of the fire. Terri never went back until Thursday to see Brittany. Terri later told me that the Doctor at the Charleston Burn Center wanted to adopt Brittany.

Rodney came out here after the fire – about two weeks after DSS took Brittany and made threats against me if I said anything bad about Terri. He'd rode past my house 2-3 times and did the same the next day. Then he came to my door. Larry was at work. It was about 2 or 3 in the afternoon. I was afraid. He knew I had talked to the SBI. He wanted to know what I had told them. He kept on and on. He was threatening me in a roundabout way. Larry came home. Larry was telling Rodney about the fire investigation. He told Rodney that Terri would walk unless someone saw Terri set the fire.

Even before Terri was pregnant with Josh, she said she was going to move to Sinkley, South Carolina, near Green Sea, close to Brittany's daddy, who killed this guy. I took that to mean Terri could get him to kill me, too, if I said the wrong thing about Terri.

The poem in the paper (about Josh). I read it when

they stayed on Wall Street after Josh was born. Terri then said her momma wrote the poem and Dana (Hammond) typed it.

Terri and Rodney moved into that house in Green Sea beside a school – same house down from Brittany's daddy. That's where they were living when Terri was arrested. This same house burned, too.

Terri and Rodney said they had complained all along about the lights flickering. They took advantage of the situation. If they had bad wiring, why didn't they tell the landlord?

All I know is that a week before the fire, Terri asked me to take Josh – you know, adopt him. I told Terri, "No." She was trying to get rid of her own son.

On September 1, 1998, Coleman interviewed Lynda Thompson, Josh's paternal grandmother. She remembered Terri and her son, Kenneth, met in the fall of 1994, while they both began taking courses at Southeastern Community College. She recalled that her son came home from classes one day saying, "I met someone at school who follows me around everywhere. I can't get rid of her."

Kenneth always had only one girlfriend at a time – altogether he'd had five by the time he met Terri. At the time, he had no friends, and no car, because he'd lost his license because of a DWI.

Kenneth was a middle child. We had always lived in Bladen County. We moved to Columbus County in 1987. Kenneth went to Christ School for the 10th and 11th grades. His father had been an alcoholic. Kenneth moved around.

He was born in 1964. He met Terri when he was 30. Terri started picking him up on her way from Fair Bluff to Hallsboro to SCC in Whiteville, and bring him home. "She was like a leech."

I didn't like her. She was poor white trash. She would leave Brittany at day-care. After bringing Kenneth home, she'd stay around in the afternoon working puzzles. I would raise cane when she left. Kenneth would say, "What can I do?" She stayed more and more. Then, she'd come over Saturdays and Sundays. She'd bring Brittany, who always had a runny nose. She'd spend the day, but I never saw Terri feed Brittany. Terri wouldn't leave until Kenneth came in for supper.

One day, I came home early. Terri was in the house. She up and tells me, "I have only one kidney and can't have any more children."

I hadn't asked, so why was she telling me about her health problems.

All of a sudden, she stopped coming. New Year's Eve they went out. Later, Kenneth told me they had sex. That was their first and only date.

The day Josh was born, Terri called me at work. "I've just given birth to your grandchild." Kenneth had gone to South Carolina to work. When he came home a few days later, I told him Terri called. He said, "The damn bitch!"

I called the hospital. Terri had said the baby was in Intensive care. The nurse said he was holding his own.

Kenneth said he'd had sex with her 2-3 times.

I called Terri at her mother's. I threatened I would get custody. "I know every judge in town."

Terri called the morning of the fire, around 8:00 am. "Lynda, I just wanted you to know before you read it in the papers that there was a fire and Josh was burned to death so you don't have to worry anymore."

I was leaning over the phone. I said, "I knew I should have gotten custody the day he was born."

Kenneth had seen Josh the morning of the blood test. DSS requested DNA testing because Terri had requested child support. Two days after the tests came back, Kenneth was Josh's dad, and Josh was dead. Later that morning, I told Kenneth Josh was dead. Kenneth let out a scream of pain and ran out into the yard where he continued screaming and cutting everything he could find with an ax.

The afternoon after the funeral, we all drove to the cemetery and had our own service. I've been to the grave many times and left flowers. I'd liked to have given my grandson a gravestone.

Terri sent a note thanking us for the flowers, saying, "It was too bad you never met Josh. He was such a beautiful child."

According to Columbus County Court records, Terri Louise Hinson filed a Mother's Affirmation of Paternity on July 22, 1996, charging Kenneth Haynes Bryant of Bladenboro, North Carolina, with being the father of Joshua Cade Hinson, DOB 5/10/95.

On October 2, 1996, (20 days before the fire which killed Josh) Terri Louise Hinson filed a Child Support Obligation/ Sole Custody Petition in which she listed NO INCOME and asked the Court that the father pay 100% of Josh's expenses, including $1,298.00 for past public assistance.

An Order of Paternity was signed by the judge on 10/7/96, but not filed until October 22, 1996, or two days after Josh's death. On November 6, 1996, a Columbus County Judge signed an Order releasing Josh's father from "paying further current support."

Coleman interviewed Betty Strickland, ex-wife of Rodney Strickland, at her home. She stated she married Rodney on August 25, 1970. "He left March 1, 1995. He walked out."

Sometime in November, my friend got a call. (My phone had been disconnected.) This lady said, "Your husband is running around. They're standing over at the phone booth right now."

Rodney came home. He denied it. Told me not to pay any attention to what I had been told.

He started staying out all night. I started keeping a

log.

Every New Year's Eve, we got together with friends before midnight. That last New Year's, he wouldn't get out of his chair. He began using any excuse to leave to go get medicine. I'd find cups in the car saying, "I love you, Dad."

I was trying to hang on to the marriage. He'd wait til I'd fallen asleep, then he'd get the keys to my car and leave.

The last day, he dropped me off – we went to Country Kitchen. I said, "Let's go to a movie and supper. He left and was gone for 1-2 weeks. I put out a APB. This was in March, 1996. He went straight to her house and he's never been back. His mother told me he's been seen with someone in a white car. (Terri Hinson's Mustang.) "He forgot all about the dinner and the movie."

Justice for Baby Josh

He and Terri would drive right by me standing at the
mailbox – me standing right there in the yard.
 I called to talk to Rodney about our oldest son. Terri
told me it was my fault.
 I used to go out with my sisters because all he
 (Rodney) wanted
to do was sit home and watch TV. I never went out without
asking if he wanted to go and I always asked him if I could go
on Ladies Night Out. "I'm a go-go. I love to dance."
 I loved him when he left. He was a fantastic husband
and father.
 After the accident on his job, his personality changed.
He became gullible, bored, and started classes at SCC. He got
lazy collecting his Workmen's Comp of $300 a week.
 One night, he told me that if I dropped the papers,
(separation/divorce) he'd come back. I told him to leave her
(Terri Hinson) like he left me. He refused.
 Rodney does not want Terri to know anything about
us – me and his two sons. Terri doesn't want Rodney to give
his sons any money. She tells him not to. If the boys ask their
father for gas money, Terri gets mad and tells him he can't.
 Whenever I call, Rodney is very cut and dry – like a
stranger. When he has visitations, he doesn't visit like he did
when Terri was in jail. He has visitations on Wednesday, 6-9
and every other weekend from Friday through Sunday. He's
never taken our teenage son Jeremy for an overnight. Rodney
and Jeremy visit back and forth between his mother's and the
trailer where we lived. Rodney has never taken Jeremy
anywhere.
 While Terri was in jail, Rodney would keep his
visitation, but he'd cut Sundays short to go visit her. As soon
as she got out, his visitations were cut way back. He won't
spend any money on Jeremy without a receipt.
 According to Columbus County Court records,

198

Bethania Durden Strickland filed a complaint for custody of a minor child, divorce "from bed and board," child support, equitable distribution of all marital assets, and alimony, on March 26, 1996, alleging that the Defendant, Rodney Strickland, "without provocation, removed himself from the marital home," that the Plaintiff "has at all times been a faithful and dutiful spouse to the Defendant and has contributed her time, energies, and efforts in establishing a home for the family... that the Defendant is currently residing in Apartment 203 Tabor Villa Apartments in Tabor City, North Carolina with another female to whom he is not married and is currently involved in an adulterous relationship with this female."

On the 25th of April, 1996, Rodney filed his Answer to the Complaint, in which he asks for joint custody of minor child, "due to the fact that the Plaintiff is not home enough to give proper guidance to the minor child, Plaintiff is not getting minor child to school on time and his spare time is being spent with friends and Plaintiff's relatives, not his mother, Plaintiff has been setting a poor example for a young child by continuing to go out to clubs for the past eight years." The Defendant also asks for "divorce from bed and breakfast," that child support payments be made through the courts," so the money won't be used "to support the Plaintiff's habit of going out to clubs," that the Defendant be given the home and the Ford Bronco acquired during the marriage, that the Defendant retain any property acquired or brought into the marriage, to have his personal belongings out of the house, that the Defendant not pay alimony "since Plaintiff earns two-thirds the amount received by the Defendant and the Plaintiff has mentioned since filing this Complaint that she may start her own cleaning business, generating even more income for her..."

Coleman finds the content and language of Rodney Strickland's Answer revealing and instructive in that Terri

Hinson boasted to Coleman that she had written the Answer
to the Complaint herself and had it notarized by a Lori A
Smith, who not only failed to properly affix her seal to the
document, if in fact, she had one issued, nor did she list her
notary number, raising the question: Was Lori A. Smith
actually Terri Hinson's sister, Linda Smith?

Coleman noted the hypocrisy, treachery, and lies Terri
Hinson wrote in the Answer, for example, that Rodney and
Terri are keeping close company solely for the purpose of
studying together, that rather than having been "shacking up,"
with Terri Hinson, Rodney "has been living with a couple
since leaving the marital home, to wit, Dana Meares and
Rocky Hammond." Terri Hinson's own track record of child
neglect, abuse, and abandonment is well–documented by her
own mother, now alleges that Mrs. Strickland is "not home
enough to give proper guidance to the minor child... that Mrs.
Strickland "has been setting a poor example for a young child
(in truth, 15 years old)..." (Talk about the pot calling the
kettle black!)

Coleman interviewed Dana Hammond at her home.
She recalled meeting Terri Hinson in algebra class in the fall
of 1993. Terri Hinson sat beside her in that class. Terri
reported being single at that time, but recounted having
problems with Phillip Gene Williams, who Terri claimed was
"following her." She only had Brittany. Dana was going
through a divorce.

Some 2-4 weeks after they had met, Terri called Dana
to come over to her mother's house to work on math. Later
we took our kids to McDonald's and went to the beach.

"There was no mother-daughter relationship – no "I
love you." If she (Terri) was agitated, she'd tell Brittany,
"Leave me alone! I don't need this!"

I'd take the kids to the play area, but Terri would stay
inside. She'd let Brittany play by herself.

Justice for Baby Josh

Terri and her mother never said, "I love you." Terri complained how her mother stayed on her case all the time, putting her down – telling Terri, "You'll never amount to anything." I asked Terri if she and her mother ever got along. She said, "No. Never."

Every time I'd be at her house, the two of them would argue constantly and cuss each other.

Terri told me to take her to have an abortion when she was pregnant with Josh. "I can't have any more kids," she told me.

Her mother confronted me at SCC and cussed me out for not telling her about Terri's pregnancy.

She'd been taking Kenneth Bryant home. He dropped out of school and set Terri up in the Tabor Villa Apartments. Social Services was paying Terri's bills. She told me, "Just go tell them you don't have a phone, a place to stay, and no income. They'll give you $350, Food Stamps, pay your light bill, HUD-paid rent, a PELL Grant, your daycare is paid for – you're crazy for not getting Social Services." Brittany was getting Social Services money for child support.

Terri told me the pictures of her children were mine. She said she'd gone to Charlotte to get an apartment and a job so she could get her kids, but when she came back, they were gone. Her mother had put them up for adoption.

About three years later, I met Anne and Richard Allen on a bus trip to Disney World. I asked them about their little boy whose leg was in a cast. I said, "He looks familiar." When we got home, I went to a florist and asked if the boy was Terri's Timothy.

The poem in the paper (*News Reporter*) about Josh 's death was written six months to a year before Josh's death, on the anniversary of his birthday. Terri had asked me to type it six months to a year before the fire.

Terri's only physical problem was while she was pregnant with Josh. One time she said, "I'm pregnant I can't have another baby. (She was 41/2 months along.) I cannot handle another baby."

I asked her if she'd thought about adoption. She said she didn't know how to go about doing it. She didn't get upset talking about it.

One time she got real mad at me because I wouldn't babysit Brittany. After that, we didn't see each other for a while.

At seven-months pregnant with Josh, she called and asked me to take her to the doctor. She told me the doctor said, "Everything's fine." We went to the mall. Terri kept looking at baby clothes. I asked her, "Are you keeping the baby?" She said, "I haven't made up my mind."

She called, "Guess what? I've had a baby. He's in the little nursery. – ICU. I'm leaving the hospital."

I offered to go get her, but she refused. She left the next afternoon. Josh stayed about a week. She only went back once or twice to see him. "I've got to go back and stay the night – I'm going to miss school," she told me.

When Josh was about a month old, and on an Apnea Monitor, she asked if I would watch the children while she was studying.

One time, we were watching TV, and the Monitor went off. Terri went over nonchalantly, turned off the Monitor, rubbed his chest, never picked him up, but put him over again.

When Josh was about four months old, Terri told me, "Don't rock him, don't you pick him up, and don't talk to him."

I never saw her rock him, cuddle him, or sing to him.

She'd told me not to get Brittany anything for Christmas (1994) that she'd have to pick up or be bothered by.

Terri would come to my house and Brittany would always want to be picked up. After that, Terri was always asking me to babysit. When Josh was 5-6 months old, Terri asked me if I would keep Josh for a little while. "I need a break." Terri wanted Rodney all to herself without his wife, his kids, or her kids. She'd said that several times over the last 6 months.

Rodney was still living with his wife. I asked Terri if she thought Rodney would leave his wife. "We can't go anywhere. He'd never say anything. Terri would tell me to leave her apartment. "Rodney is coming."

He showed her attention. One time my friend and I were studying and Terri would get right between us, she couldn't stand me having another friend. Later, Terri started bad-mouthing my friend. She couldn't stand me even talking to other women or friends.

She took Josh everywhere. She said she didn't want Kenny's mother to find him and take him away.

I saw Terri 30 minutes before the car incident. She had Josh with her. She called me later that afternoon after I'd got home and said DSS was going to take Josh because she'd left Josh in the car unattended. She asked to use me as a reference. DSS questioned me. I said, I'd never known her to leave the baby.

Terri smoked all the time she was pregnant. She smoked during the time Josh was on the Monitor. She always smoked around the baby.

She drank coffee and tea. Terri said his medicine had caffeine because of all the caffeine she drank while she was pregnant with Josh.

I told Terri to stop smoking but she said, "I smoked during all the other pregnancies." (Perhaps that's why she had so many low birth weight babies, so many miscarriages, and so many children with learning and neurological problems!) In addition to Josh, Bradley Tripp was diagnosed with congenital encephalopathy "based on prematurity." (Why hadn't DSS forced Terri to have her tubes tied?)

Justice for Baby Josh

The reason I was never in Terri's house on Wall Street was because of the car insurance mess. Terry put her car on my insurance and I got stuck paying after she promised to pay.

The next time I went to Wall Street, it was to get my typewriter. Terri met me at the door because "Rodney was in a mood.'

I remember Terri would get upset when Rodney went to see Jeremy, his teenage son. She had asked me about how I felt about my husband visiting his daughter. She said, "It aggravates me when Rodney goes when I've fixed supper."

Terri would get upset because he'd left her that night. (The night of the fire) Terri was convinced Vick, Rodney's oldest son, was following her.

One time Terri said Rodney wished Josh was his, but he told me in private he didn't want to have to raise any more kids. "I've had my family. I'll help Terri raise hers, but I don't want anymore."
He'd play with Josh and Brittany. Terri never would. If Rodney was out playing in the yard with the kids, Terri would tell him to come in and do something for her.

Rodney would get up with the kids at night. Her kids were always sick. She wouldn't stay home. "I hate to miss a day of school," she'd say as an excuse for not staying home with her sick kids. She had Medicaid.

One day I asked her, "Terri, are you taking the kids to the hospital because they're sick or because you need attention?" She cussed me out.

The night of the fire, she called me around 5:00-5:30 am. "Damn it, Terri, why are you calling?"

"I have something to tell you," she said. She didn't seem upset. "I wanted to tell you before you heard it from someone else."

I said, "Terri, hold on a minute."

She says, "Josh died. this morning."

"Josh who," I asked.

"My Josh."

I ask, "You're telling me there was a fire in the house? Where's Brittany?"

"She's in the hospital. She's at Loris on the way to Charleston. They didn't think she was burned. I'm on my way to Mamma's."

Terri never said where she was calling from. I was in tears.

Terri said, "Well, it's something we can't help."

I thought she was in shock. I drove to her mother's in Fair Bluff. Got there around 7:00 am -- 5-6 people were there. Rodney and Terri were sitting on the couch. Terri was wearing a long sleeve flannel shirt, with her arms around her knees. She looked up. "It's alright," she said, "last night, Rodney was at his mom's for visitation with his son." Terri said she had two heaters running. (I'd never been inside the house.) "I woke up hearing Brittany scream. I went upstairs and couldn't see anything. I went back downstairs and called 911. Went back inside the house and went upstairs. I went inside Josh's bedroom and a ball of flames shot from his closet. I kept calling. I hear him say, "Mommy! Mommy!" I couldn't breathe, I went downstairs. The fire department was there." (Terry showed no tears. Her eyes were not watering. She didn't seem as if she'd been crying. No puffiness around her eyes.)

Terri told me they were taking Brittany to Charleston and had revived her on the way to the hospital.

I asked if Terri was going to Charleston.

Terri said, "No, not today. Somebody's going, but we're not sure yet."

I could smell smoke. Her face and arms were clean. One leg was sun-dyed. She said she had her clothes on before the fire. I'd never known her to sleep in her clothes. I'd been at her apartment at 10:00 PM and she'd be in a nightgown and robe. "What did you sleep in last night?"

She answered, "The clothes I got on."

I'd probably been with her some 100 evenings over five years and she'd always change into a gown and robe.

She kept scratching the back of her hand. and she coughed a couple of times when lighting a cigarette. She said she was fine. Her head looked like some trash or fine bits of ash. Her hair was singed in a line from her crown backward.

"I want to get up," she said. We went outside.

People started coming in after lunch. It was a tense mood. Nobody knew what to say. Terri would cry – tear up when family members would come over, but as soon as they'd walk away, she'd stop.

I went home, fixed lunch for my family, then went back over to Terri's. When Rocky and I arrived, Terri had changed her clothes and taken a bath. She'd washed her hair. Rodney and Terri asked me to fix her hair. Her eyebrows and hair on her arms were not singed.

I told Rock, "She just didn't act right."

Bernice was hateful. She'd get mad at anyone who showed Terri sympathy.

The only times I saw Terri sad was at the funeral home and at the funeral.

I'd only cut her hair one time at the school. April Crabtree had cut her hair two weeks earlier. She cut Josh's, too. April doesn't work Monday. On Monday, the day after the fire, I went to Terri mother's in Fair Bluff. Terri looked tired. She had to make funeral arrangements. People were bringing flowers, food, toys for Brittany. I noticed Terri's hair was only singed in one area – her crown to hairline in front three inches wide. Terri said she wasn't bent over. I called Andra Smith, SCC cosmetology instructor, who said they used mannequins, a cigarette lighter, and a metal pail to singe hair. Did the same with lighter and singed a wide band.

Tuesday, I curled her hair at her mother's house.

Around 5:00 PM, we went to the funeral home where Terri laid across the casket and screamed for an hour. The funeral home had said there wasn't enough left of Josh to dress. Terry was irate with Rodney for not dressing Josh.

When we left the funeral home, Terri was laughing. and joking about the flowers (clown flowers).

Wednesday, the day of the funeral, the *Tribune* article said arson was suspected.

Terri and her mother had argued the day before.

We went back to the house. Terri was saying, "This is going to ruin my name." She was trying to convince us she didn't set the fire. Her family was in the kitchen. Terri and her mother were arguing about lawyers. Terri wanted to sue attorney Richard Wright and Mr. Jones, the two owners of the house. Terri said it was the heater that caused the fire. She couldn't get Josh's door open. Then the door was open and she got too close to the fire. It shocked me. She's just buried her child. The last thing I'd be worried about would be suing.

Rocky and I went to Charleston either the next Saturday or Sunday. Terri, her mother, and Rodney were there. Brittany asked if she could come home with me. Terri called and said DSS was putting Brittany in protective custody. Brittany had been told Josh is "in heaven."

Terri called from time to time asking me to take Brittany. I said, "Yes," but you've got to visit when they say."

I went with her to the Hearing. The night before, Terri had asked me to testify that I'd been in the house. (Terri drew me a picture of Josh's room and the water stain on his ceiling. Terri got mad when I refused to lie. Then, she asked me for a pacifier necklace to make her look good at the Hearing.

My mother was on the phone with Terri, who was saying, "I'm going to own Jones' Stores I'm going to sue Richard Wright and Mr. Jones." Terri said she had already contacted attorneys in Fayetteville.

Later, Terri told me she failed a lie detector test because "I was nervous."

The church had given her $500 for clothes for Brittany and herself. She used the money to pay for the lie detector test, which she said she failed. "I'm going to take another one."

A week or two after the fire, Terri called and asked to use our pick-up to move her stuff out of the Wall Street burned house. "Can you help us move?'

On the way to pick up the truck, Terri claimed the SBI was following her. Terri and Rodney came and went across the police lines removing stuff from the house.

On the way back, I asked about Brittany. Terri said, "I've got something to tell you. The day before the fire, I told him (Rodney) not to leave, (go to his ex-wife's for visitation with his son Jeremy). I told him if he left something would happen and it did. I told Rodney if he left the house that night something would happen."

"Terri, what are you saying?"

"You know what I'm saying."

I made her stop and I got out. I got sick.

"What's wrong with you?'

"It's my stomach." I was sitting on the ground. She told me to get back in the car. She began talking chit-chat as if nothing happened.

"Now, when they call you from the SBI, you don't talk to them.

As I got out, I said, "Don't come back! Leave me alone!"

Terri got mad, "What's wrong with you?"

Rodney said, "She needs you."

"No, she doesn't. Leave me out of it."

Terri told me to keep my remarks to myself. She had invited me to chicken that night. She had been up in the children's rooms while moving stuff that afternoon. She had told me about the position of Josh in his bed. (How did she know? It was a fireman who found him.)

In jail, Terri told me the reason she wrote to me telling me what to say was, "You've never been in trouble, never done anything wrong, and they'd believe you."

Outside jail, Rodney said, "All this is real hard on her."

Now, as I started to leave without staying for the chicken dinner, Rodney grabbed me by the coat and said, "Don't do this to her."

The next thing I know, Rodney, Bernice, and Terri's sister Linda start calling – threatening me.

One evening, I heard a car pull up. Rodney was at the door. He opened the door. He had a cigar and my chain.

"Come on in."

"I wanted to give this back to you," he said handing me my chain. "Don't accuse her – "He knocked on my wall and said, "This could go up any minute." He then put his hand on my child's head.

Rodney kept calling – about 8-10 times. Once he came to the house. "I'll kill anyone who testifies against Terri. I believe her and you better believe her too, or else."

Terry's sister Linda got a job at a trailer place where I was trying to buy a trailer and suddenly fictitious bad credit started showing up on bank drafts being made on my account, like a $5,000 furniture repo.

Coleman followed up with a visit to Tracy Wilson of UFS Trailers, who said, "No, I don't want it printed that I had anything to do with it." (Dana's credit report.) It was reported that Terri's sister, Linda, left the next day for Charlotte and hasn't been back.

Coleman learned that Terri Hinson was administered a polygraph test on March 17, 1998, by Joseph Kenny, of Kenny & Associates, PO Box 32812, Charlotte, NC 28232, (704) 552-4804. In his interview with Terri Hinson's closest confident, Dana Hammond, Coleman learned that Terri had confided that she flunked the polygraph because "I was nervous."

Tabor City Fire Chief Jerry Watts told Coleman that neither he nor any of his volunteer firemen had any doubts that Terri Hinson set the fire the early morning of October 20, 1996, which resulted in the death of her infant son and would have killed her daughter, if his firemen had not rescued her as soon as they did. Chief Watts was on the stairs with his firemen first tried to get up the stairs. "The bedroom door at the head of the stairs was closed. No doubt about it." When asked why she had not been convicted, Chief Watts opined that no one bothers to take a small-town volunteer fire department seriously.

A Summary of The Results of Coleman's Six-Month Investigation

1. **The 911 Call.** Terri Hinson's recorded voice on her 911 call was shrill, loud, hard, but dry and void of sobbing, or grieving. Furthermore, she yelled to the Dispatcher, "My kids are upstairs and I can't get them." Yet, she would later tell law enforcement that she went back upstairs after going downstairs to get her phone to make the 911 call and that she was upstairs while making the 911 call. In fact, she tells the 911 dispatcher, "I can't even get upstairs." That sounds as if she hasn't tried to get upstairs. Yet, she would later insist that she had gone upstairs to try to rescue both Brittany and Josh. If she had tried to save the children, wouldn't she tell the Dispatcher that fact in order to convey her desperation?

"My house is engulfed in flames," Terri Hinson claims to the Dispatcher. "Engulfed," seems to be a formal, contrived word out of context with the dire circumstances being described.

Then, Terri Hinson repeats, "I can't even get

upstairs," this second time seeming to be an excuse for not trying to save her children.

"It's coming through the kitchen!" There was never any evidence that fire reached the kitchen or even that the room above the kitchen. (The master bedroom sustained no damage other than a suspicious charred spot on Terri Hinson's bed which only one fire investigator reported without further noting that multiple origins are common in arson.)

Next, Terri Hinson yells five times, "Oh God, my young-uns are gone! My young-uns are gone! My babies are gone! Oh, they're gone! My babies are gone!" In truth, the only way she could have known her children were dead was that either she had waited to call 911 until she believed it was too late to save her children, and/or that she had wanted them dead and was "hoping out loud," a common phenomenon for the most uncommon of acts, to wit, a mother killing her children.

Seconds later, she's talking to the police at her front who have just arrived. "Straight in – one's to the left and one's straight in ...Both of them." She had told Coleman, "I couldn't breathe. I ran downstairs for the phone and while calling, went back upstairs. When I saw the blue lights (police cars), I ran downstairs... The two officers pulled me out of the house." According to the 911 recorded call, none of what she told Coleman was true. At all times during the 911 call, she says she is downstairs and can't get upstairs.

2. **The Initial Fire Scene**. Both Tabor City Police Officers Russell and Moyer reported that the house upstairs windows were black, smoke was rising from the back of the house, and the only light was from a downstairs light. As they approached the front of the house, a woman opened the door. She was fully dressed, including shoes and socks, was wearing glasses, and carrying a cigarette case in one hand and

holding a cordless phone in the other, on which she was talking.

If there was no sign of flames from the upstairs windows, and as yet, no signs of flames when the front door opened, how did Terry Hinson report that the house was "engulfed in flames, unless she had set the fire in Josh's bedroom, waited for the fire to get blazing enough to close the door to Josh's bedroom, and then go downstairs to call 911?

Why would Terri Hinson be fully dressed at 3:58 AM Sunday morning, including socks, shoes, glasses, cigarette case, and phone unless she was making sure she could get out of the house in time to save herself and her necessities?

As noted earlier, but would seem worth repeating, in Dr. Hurst's investigative report 18 months after the fire, Hurst listed the following "potential factors (in arson cases) not related to combustion"... (1) remote location, (2) fire near service equipment or appliance, (3) removal or replacement of goods, (4) absence of personal items, (5) entry blocked or obstructed, (6) sabotage to structure or fire protection, and damage to fire-resistive assemblies, and (7) open windows and exterior doors," asserting that, "None of the elements of the three categories recognized by the NFPA as indicative of arson is present in this case."

In his rush to prove Terri Hinson's innocence, Dr. Hurst overlooked the following contradictions to his own conclusions:

a. The consensus was that the fire originated in the closet in the far-left corner of Josh's bedroom. This would seem to meet the test of Dr. Hurst's "remoteness."

b. There was an electrical outlet in Josh's closet which Terri regularly used to do her ironing, and a Romex cable overhead, which would meet Hurst's requirement of fire being "near service equipment."

c. By removing baseboard heat as a heating source

that night of the fire, using the portable heaters at their maximum capacity, and placing the heaters up and downstairs AFTER claiming to have observed electrical problems following Hurricane Fran, Terri Hinson contrived to divert the cause of the fire from Josh's closet to the portable heaters, thereby satisfying the potential non-combustible factor of "removal or replacement of goods."

d. How could Hurst have missed the evidence right under his nose – eyes -- that Terri Hinson had removed personal items from being damaged by the fire? She had, in fact, removed her most personal item – HERSELF, along with her glasses, her cigarettes and case, her clothing, and her cordless phone. And rather than go immediately to the hospital in Charleston where Brittany had been airlifted, she and her boyfriend are back at the house two hours after the fire, crossing police crime scene tapes to load more personal items into their car. (Come-on Dr. Hurst; you're playing the game of life and death with a marked deck of cards.)

e. The police and firemen looked for an alternative to the front door entrance. The only other entrance was a side door locked and blocked by a table, thereby being another example of meeting Hurst's tests of potential arson, "entry blocked or obstructed."

f. Officer Ramey, who had rented the Wall Street property before Terri Hinson and Rodney Strickland, had told Lt. Glenn and Coleman that he had purchased smoke detectors and placed them throughout the house, upstairs and downstairs. Yet, at the time of the fire, no smoke detectors were found, leading one to conclude that either Officer Ramey had lied, or that Terri Hinson or Rodney Strickland had removed the smoke detectors prior to setting the fire., and by their actions, had met yet another test of being arson suspects, "sabotage to structure or fire protection."

Finally, Dr. Hurst's criteria for suspecting arson includes

213

evidence of "opening of windows and exterior doors," in other words, an attempt to control the amount of air available to the fire. Terri Hinson initially claimed that the "doors to the children's bedrooms were always open," then stated she didn't know how Josh's bedroom could have been closed, changed her statement again, saying she closed his door because of the "excessive heat" from the heater in the hall outside his door. She did say that earlier that night, she had heard "Josh cry" and had taken a flashlight upstairs to check on him around 10:30. She never mentioned closing his door at that time, nor does she say she went upstairs at any time after that. Yet, the police officers and firemen independently reported seeing flames under Josh's bedroom door, meaning his door was closed by the time, if not just before, Terri Hinson reported the fire. She also admitted Josh's door was "extremely hard to open or close," which would eliminate Brittany as being the person who closed his bedroom door. With closing the door because of the "excessive heat" going into his room, being a specious and implausible reason – why wasn't Brittany's door also closed as the heater was purportedly placed in the hall to heat both rooms equally, or more plausibly, the heater turned down or off? The only credible explanation is that the door was open when she set the fire in his closet, kept open to ventilate the fire, and then closed to make sure Josh died in the fire.

Similarly, Terri Hinson noted the downstairs heater was "cold" when she moved it out of the way for the police to enter the house. Yet, fire investigators two days later noted the heater setting was set at its highest reading. Again, the only reasonable explanation is that Terri Hinson opened the front door to create an air flow up the stairs and into Josh's bedroom and his closet, while forgetting that the air coming in the front door would cool the downstairs heater sitting in the open doorway, a complication she would have to try to explain away.

In any event, it is apparent from Terri Hinson's misstatements, contractions, and changed accounts, that doors had been manipulated to maximize and control the fire, just as Hurst described in his profile of an arsonist's fire-setting behavior.

In conclusion, rather than stating that "none" of the indicators of arson were present in the Hinson case, Dr. Hurst should have written, "ALL of the indicators of arson were present in the Hinson case." But then, Dr. Hurst had made up his mind before he bought his plane ticket in Texas that Terri Hinson did not set the fire, so he was predisposed to ignore culpable evidence. Shame on you Dr. Hurst for violating the most fundamental principle of any investigation – a pre-existing.

3. **What Did Terry Hinson Do To Try to Save Josh and Brittany?** To the 911 Dispatcher Terri Hinson yells, "My kids are upstairs and I can't get them!... I can't even get upstairs! My babies are gone." ... Then, while still connected to 911, she tells Officer Russell and Moyer, "Straight in both of them...they can't get to them." When officer Russell and Moyer return from trying to find another way into the house, they reported Terri Hinson was as they had left her, talking on her phone.

The obvious conclusions are: (1) From the time Terri Hinson made the 911 call at 3:57 AM, she made no attempt to go upstairs, and (2) By admitting to the Dispatcher, "I can't get them... I can't even get up the stairs," she unwittingly admitted she had not tried.

Yet, two days later, she would tell SBI Agent Matt White, "I heard Brittany calling, 'Mamma, I'm scared!' That when Terri Hinson opened her eyes, she saw a "reddish/orange glow coming from upstairs." (Not possible from where she reports being positioned on the couch around the corner from the stairs with Josh's door being closed.)

Justice for Baby Josh

At another time, she claims she heard the crackling of the fire. She ran upstairs and ducked down at the landing. She says Josh's door is open. (Police and firemen reported Josh's door to be closed.) When she gets to the doorjamb area, "The fire goes whoosh". (Terri Hinson must have been planning this fire for months as she had (1) obtained books about arson investigations, and (2) she had questioned her best friend's boyfriend, himself a fireman, on the phenomenon of a fire's "rollover" and the sound it makes.)

She said felt the heat coming out of the room (Josh's). The fire came out above her head and singed her hair. (SBI Agent Matt White does not see any burns or singed hair. Hinson explains she had a friend fix her hair before the interview. (The mother of a four-year-old daughter coming back from near death at a hospital in Charleston, is home getting her hair fixed! Why the rush? Because she had "singed" her hair with the curling iron she'd used to fix her mother's hair earlier that night? Hadn't a member of the Rescue Squad reported that the "singed hair" appeared in a curious straight line? Hadn't the friend who fixed her hair the day after the fire told Coleman that Terri's hair was singed in a straight line three inches wide?" Hmmm.)

The mother says she tried to get to her daughter, but her room was too full of smoke. Twice, she hears Josh call, "Mamma." She says she couldn't get in the room because the fire was coming out of Josh's closet and spreading. (Her claim that Josh called her twice, seconds before she called 911, is further contradicted by the evidence of complete charring on Josh's body. Josh couldn't have cried "Mamma," because he was already dead.

Brittany keeps saying, "I'm scared." The mother reports she told her daughter to come to her, but she wouldn't.

Brittany didn't come to her mother because her mother never went upstairs to try to save her. Instead,

Brittany was found lifeless on the floor trying to crawl under her bed.

Next, she tells SBI Agent White that she went downstairs and grabbed the cordless phone, called 911, then went back upstairs with the phone. (On the tape of the 911 call, Hinson states she's downstairs and can't get upstairs to get the children. Terri Hinson never went back upstairs while, or after, calling 911. In fact, she admitted to the Dispatcher, "I can't even get upstairs."

Hinson says the 911 Dispatcher told her to get out of the house. (Not according to the tape. Besides, she was in the house when the police arrived.)

Terri next tells SBI Agent White that she noticed a police car next door. (Because she was watching instead of trying to get to her children.)

"The downstairs heater was in the way of the front door, so I grabbed it to let the policeman enter. The heater is cold because the power has gone off." (No, the light in the living room where she was standing when the police arrived, was on!)

Another time, she told investigators that she went upstairs and told Brittany "to run." A curious and suspect instruction. "Run"? Why didn't her mother tell her daughter to get on the floor and crawl toward the door some four or five feet away? Or, the question of questions, why didn't Terri Hinson crawl toward her daughter a few feet away, and pull her to safety?

Because, as Terri Hinson admitted, "I can't even get up the stairs!" She lied. She never tried to save either Brittany or Josh. The only way such a conclusion makes sense is she set the fire to get rid of her children and she certainly wasn't going to risk her life to undue months of planning. Did Susan Smith jump in John D. Long Lake to save her two sons she had buckled into their car seats and driven the car into the lake?

4. The Rescue of Brittany and Recovery of Josh.

All of those present when Brittany and Josh were brought out of the burning house reported that Terri Hinson never made an attempt to go to her children in the ambulances, never inquired as their status, and, in fact refused invitations to ride in the ambulance with either child, first telling Rescue Squad staffer Lorrie Lancaster, "I'm waiting for my boyfriend," and then repeating the same to ambulance driver Sykes, who was ready to rush Josh to the hospital.

The only explanation for such callous disregard for her children and such a reprehensible preference for her boyfriend is that Terri Hinson had set the fire to get rid of her children in order to secure her relationship with her boyfriend, who had made it known he'd already raised two children of his own and had no desire to raise someone else's.

In fact, Terri Hinson would later confess to friend Dana Hammond that she had threatened to "make something bad happen" if Rodney left that weekend to spend time over at his ex-wife's house with their teenage son. When asked by Dana Hammond, "Terri, what are you saying," Terri admitted that the "something bad" was the fire? Terri Hinson had admitted she set the fire!

Afterward, Rodney Strickland threatened to set Dana's residence on fire and to "kill anyone who testified against Terri."

By her singular statement, "I'm waiting for my boyfriend," Terry Hinson not only confessed to Josh's murder, the attempted murder of Brittany, and First Degree Arson, she defined her motive: She got rid of her children to secure her relationship with Rodney Strickland." (Susan Smith and Diane Downs had done the same and for the same reason.)

5. Terri Hinson's Explanation as to the Cause of

the Fire. Three hours after the fire, Terri Hinson and Rodney Strickland were discovered crossing the crime scene tape to remove items from the burned residence. Ordered to the police station to explain why they had violated the police tape, Terri Hinson told Lt. Glenn, "I intentionally sleep downstairs because the electrical plug on the heater might spark ... the (heater) wire felt hot before the fire started." During the fire, she had told Lt. Glenn, "Someone told me the fire was electrical." Minutes before, she told Trooper Lewis, she fell asleep downstairs because there was something electrical downstairs she didn't trust. The day after the fire, she reported to SBI Agent Matt White, "I stayed downstairs because the heater downstairs might catch fire." Two days after the fire, Terri Hinson told investigators Mathews and Magini, "I didn't use baseboard heat because it is dangerous," then, that same day, explained to Agent White again, she didn't want to sleep upstairs because she didn't trust the downstairs heater. Four days after the fire, she informed Dept of Social Services worker Baldwin, that Hurricane Fran had caused electrical problems, so the night of the fire, she slept downstairs in case the heater "might catch fire." In July, 1998, or nearly two years after the fire, Terri Hinson told Coleman, "Both heaters were on high... the curling iron stopped working ... both cords were hot ...I decided to sleep on the couch to be there near the outlet in case anything happened."

Yet, Terri Hinson had also told these same people, "I saw fire coming from the closet (in Josh's upstairs bedroom.) So why, did she try to persuade everyone that the downstairs heater was the cause of the fire, while at the same time claiming to have seen the fire confined to Josh's bedroom closet?

First, by claiming the heater downstairs posed an imminent danger, she believed law enforcement would not be suspicious as to her being fully dressed, wearing shoes, socks, her glasses, her cigarette case in one hand and a cordless phone in the other, when the police, firefighters, and Rescue Squad arrived. Second, to throw investigators off her trail, she had to continually spin the "electrical problem," as the cause of the fire. In fact, she was so brazen as to tell Lt. Glenn, while the fire was still being fought, that, "Someone told me the fire was electrical – caused by the heater upstairs," which she knew to be a lie because, at that point, she'd had no discussion with anyone as to the cause of the fire.

Or, was she trying to sway law enforcement that both heaters, ironing cords, and curling irons had exacerbated electrical problems resulting from Hurricane Fran?

But, NEMAX fire investigators, two days after the fire, found the downstairs heater set on 1,500 amps, its maximum output, with the dial on "9," also its maximum. So, why would Terri Hinson, who worked so hard to convince law enforcement that she didn't trust the heater downstairs have put herself and her children in danger by using that heater at all, and then turn it on so as to maximize the danger?

The problem for Terri Hinson was that she was attempting to use the downstairs heater as both her cover for sleeping downstairs fully dressed, and be the cause of the fire, thereby tripping over her lies on both counts.

For example, she admitted the downstairs heater was "cold" when she picked it up to move it so the police could go up the stairs to try to rescue Josh and Brittany, yet NEMAX found the same heater's settings on their highest readings and the light (electricity) on in the living room when the police arrived. The only way the heater could have cooled, was that (1) Terry Hinson had never plugged in the heater, (2) she had earlier unplugged the heater, or most credible, (3) she had unplugged the heater when she opened the front door to vent the fire upstairs and was watching out the window while on the phone to 911, to have the door closed when the police turned the corner. (The transcript of the 911 call and Officer's Russell and Moyer reports show she was at the door and on the 911 call when the police arrived.)

Only the pomp and bluster of Dr. Hurst's ego-engineered con of the Columbus County District Attorney, already looking for a way to avoid bringing a Columbus County mom to trial, lest her incur the displeasure of woman voters in his County, and certainly their wrath, if he lost, was ready and eager to trump the preponderance of compelling physical and circumstantial evidence pointing to her guilt gathered by the State, with Hurst's flawed, bogus, and biased report. Poof! Out the window with the state's evidence, and out the door walked Terri Louise Hinson, freed by a District Attorney who placed political gain over protecting the public. She had done that which Susan Smith, Diane Downs, and Dr. Greene had failed to do. She had gotten by with the murder of her child.

Coleman v Hinson for the Murder of Josh Hinson

Terri had a history of neglecting her children, abandoning her children, and disposing of her children. (She signed papers to have her first three children adopted. Court records prove her claim that DSS took her children from her while she was out of town, to be a lie.)

Terri's own mother had earlier reported Terri to DSS for not being a suitable mother. Neighbors, husbands, fathers of her children, boyfriend's, and best friends had independently recalled instances in which they observed Terri Hinson being guilty of cruelty, abuse, and gross neglect of all her children. She had confided to friends she wanted to abort Josh. She had asked friends to "take" Josh – informally adopt him.

In short, Terri Hinson had given birth to five children, only to fail each and every one of them according to minimal standards of mothering – worse – she found them expendable as soon as they interfered with her quest to have a man in her life to control.

Second, Josh's paternal grandmother, described to Coleman, how Terri had suddenly volunteered that, due to her having lost a kidney to surgery, she could not have any children. This was during a time when Terri was making a nuisance of herself by hanging around in an effort to win the heart, mind, and inheritance of Josh's father-to-be. Terri had of course lied. She had, a second time, conned a pregnancy for profit.

At seven months pregnant with Josh, she called her friend Dana Hammond, to take her to the doctor, who told her, "everything's fine." Terri and Dana went to the mall. Terri kept looking at baby's clothes. Dana asked her, "Are you keeping the baby?" She said, "I haven't made up my mind."

A few weeks later, Terri called Dana. "Guess what? I've had a baby. He's in the little nursery – ICU. I'm leaving the hospital." Dana offered to come to give Terri a ride home. Eager to get away and leave her new baby behind, Terri declined. The hospital would later call DSS to come get the baby as the mother seems to have left it.

Undeterred by the fact she had driven Josh's father away by her possessiveness, Terri had called Josh's grandmother soon after delivery to announce she had just given birth to her grandson.

It wasn't until Josh's grandmother, having already witnessed Terri's neglect of Brittany, offered to take Josh, that Terri, out of spite, decided to keep Josh.

When Josh was about four months old, Terri instructed her friend Betty Gore, "Don't rock him, don't you pick him up, and don't talk to him."

So why didn't Terry let her grandmother have Josh? Because the purpose of having Josh was to guarantee Terri her place in the Big House. So, if she were to give grandmother custody of Josh, Terri's efforts would have been for naught and Terri would be left outside looking in, again.

On the other hand, Josh's health problems cramped Terri's style in general, and her new relationship with Rodney Strickland, who had a lump sum Workmen's Comp settlement on the horizon.

Do you see where Terri's heading? One fortune lost, another found. Well, not so easily obtained. Rodney was married and had two sons, one in his twenties, and the other a mid-teen. Rodney had already raised two sons, and let Terri know, he didn't want to raise someone else's.

Terri never met a man, or a relationship, she couldn't control, at least for a while – usually a very short while, but she wasn't one to take responsibility for her past. First things first: Get rid of Rodney's wife. Slander, brainwashing, and drafting Rodney's Separation Agreement would do.

Meanwhile, Josh needs constant attention, his breathing needs to be monitored, his nose is always running, he keeps an incessant cold, she can't just dump him in daycare like she can with Brittany, she can't take him to class, all the while, keeping Rodney in tow, which causes its own form of possessive monitoring.

Josh has got to go. Adoption? No, he's too sickly. Who would want him?

A week before the fire, Terri asks her close friend Betty Gore to take –adopt Josh. Betty declines. Terri had previously asked Dana Hammond to adopt Brittany, who had tentatively agreed, but only if Terri would keep in constant contact according to DSS rules.

Terri's life is beginning to unravel. Even though she's milking the State of North Carolina, and the Federal Government with every kind of Welfare and School grant she can finagle, she can't bring Josh to school, and she's already been caught once leaving Josh alone in the car. Rodney is still unwilling to marry her with two kids in the way, and he keeps insisting on having his visitations at his ex-wife's house, which a possessive control freak like Terri finds intolerable.

Besides, one of the landlords at 101 Wall Street is a well-known attorney and the other is a wealthy store owner. It's a very old house. The light fixtures seem ancient, like they are looking for a fire to happen. Terri sees a gold mine, where others saw only a 55-year-old house.

October, 1996. Despite all Terri's efforts to split asunder Rodney's relationship with his teenage son, and her unsuccessful attempts to get Rodney to say, "I do," on Saturday, October 19, 1996, Rodney announces he is leaving for Fair Bluff to go to his ex-wife's for a weekend visitation with his son.

Terri Hinson feels threatened – No, Terri Hinson is enraged. She has warned Rodney that something "bad" is going to happen if he leaves. He leaves anyway. Torments of torments -- Terri Hinson has lost control. Somebody is going to pay.

Terri had been reading books on arson, asking friends questions about "rollover," planning how to set the fire, how to make it appear as if it were caused by electrical malfunction, and ultimately, how to get rid of Josh, gain control of Rodney Strickland, profit from Strickland's Workman's Comp Settlement, get even richer by suing her wealthy landlords for wrongful death of her children, and get even with Josh's grandmother for having made her feel unwanted – not good enough for her son.

The baseboard heat could not be manipulated, but the portable heaters could be by placing them anywhere. The heaters could then be blamed with overloading the out-dated system. Add Hurricane Fran to the equation, and the possibilities can be made to seem downright plausible.

Sometime after finishing talking on the phone to her

brother around 11:00 PM, Terri used the curling iron to make her hair appear to be singed. In the dark who would notice? If push comes to shove, she'll get her friend and hairdresser, Dana Hammond to fix her hair to remove any suspicion.

But, staying awake might be a problem. Smoking and drinking tea or coffee being her "speed' of choice. She would report having trouble sleeping that night. (Planning to torch your own children can cause even the evilest among us to have trouble sleeping -- so would making sure you get out of the burning house in time.) The solution? Say you fell asleep on the couch fully dressed, and hope the cops don't find out from your friends that they have never seen you at night without sleeping garment and robe.

Around three or three thirty, Terri takes the flashlight so as to be sure not to wake the children by turning on the stairway light, and tip-toes up the stairs. (She'd later claim there was no light switch on the stairs, but Coleman has a picture of just such a light switch at the bottom of the stars.)

Josh's closet is the place of choice because: (1) It is remote, (2) There are loose hanging dresses in the closet which would ignite with a cigarette lighter, (3) There is an outlet in the closet and therefore wires overhead which, if overheated, could be blamed for the fire.(4) She can work in there without waking Josh, and (5) It has the greatest chance of achieving her goal, to wit, finally getting rid of Josh.

Using her cigarette lighter, Terri Hinson sets fire to one or more of her hanging dresses. Once satisfied the fire would do its mischief, she closes only the left of the two closet doors but leaves Josh's bedroom door open for maximum ventilation.

She then goes into her bedroom where she tries to set fire to her bed in order to detract from her intention to murder her son. (NEMAX would notice the small isolated area of burning on Terri's bed, but ignored its significance as a calling card for arson.) Terri Hinson then goes back downstairs, where she opens the front door to increase the chimney effect, thereby cooling off the heater at the foot of the stairs.

As soon as she hears the cracking fire, she goes up the stairs, observes the amount of flames shooting up through the ceiling in Josh's closet, concludes the fire is going strong enough to close Josh's door as much as the carpet will allow, then quietly and quickly goes back downstairs where she waits– waits for Josh and Brittany to die.

She may or may not have heard Brittany cry, "Mommy, I'm scared," unless she did while she was closing Josh's door. Certainly, she never heard Josh. If she was upstairs, when Brittany called her, and she ignored her... that's too evil to contemplate, unless one considers that Dr. Green torched the stairway while her children slept in their upstairs bedrooms. The only child of three to have survived managed to crawl out her bedroom onto the roof. Dr. Greene told her daughter to jump into her arms but then withdrew her arms as her child plunged to the ground.

When, or if Brittany, called out, is unknown. Terri's implausible instructions for Brittany to "run," is absurd on its face, and would lead us to believe, Terri did nothing to try to save Brittany, which would fit the fact that the fireman who rescued Brittany found her face down on her bedroom floor as if she had been trying to save herself by crawling under her bed.

If on the other hand, the fire or smoke was now severe enough to escape from Josh's closed door into Brittany's room, causing Brittany to cry, it meant her mission was accomplished and it was time to call 911, which she did.

While on the phone to the 911 dispatcher, Officers Moyer and Russell, who arrive. As they rush to the front door, Terri Hinson opens the door, fully dressed in jeans, t-shirt, shoes, socks, wearing her glasses, carrying her cigarette case in one hand and her cordless phone in the other, behaving just as Dr. Hurst described every arsonist behaves: She has removed her personal items –especially herself, from being destroyed in the fire. (Those not removed before the fire will be immediately removed after the fire, and BEFORE the mother visits her dying daughter in the Burn Center Hospital in Charleston, South Carolina.)

Now, all that was left, was to convince the local cops the volunteer firemen that the fire was caused by faulty wiring in this 55-year-old house, which should be "a piece of cake." After all, she'd been taking a course in criminal justice at Southeastern Community College, which was probably more than the local cops had done, and she's done her homework – she even found out about the "roll-over" and the "woosh" sound it makes.

And Terri was a life-long liar – 30 years of lying should hold her in good stead.

1. She'd gotten rid of Josh, who had not only failed to get his father to marry her, and admission into the Big House, but who had now become too burdensome to bear.
2. Unfortunately, Brittany had survived, but 50% ain't half bad, and with Josh gone, she was 50% closer to getting Rodney to marrying her, in turn, getting her hands on the $20,000 Workman's Comp settlement.
3. As a grieving mother, she now has 100% control of Rodney, thereby putting the final nail in his ex-wife's coffin,
4. She gets to sue her two rich landlords, for the wrongful death of Josh, and injuries to Brittany, and with her winnings, finally gets to live in her own Big House,
5. She gets even with Josh's snobby grandmother, to wit, telling her "Josh is dead; Now, you'll

227

never be able to win by getting him away from me!"

6. Terri Louise Hinson finally achieves celebrity status in a town which had always considered the Hinsons "poor white trash."

Josh's death was a win, win, win, win, win, win, situation for Terri Hinson. A mom's perfect murder.

Baby Josh Cade Hinson, conceived by his mother to dupe his father into marrying her, in turn, being used by his mother to gain "forced entrance" into the Big House and upper-middle class status for her who was born into "southern white trash." Baby Josh, neglected *in utero* by his mother, who continued to consume nicotine throughout the pregnancy, thereby dooming Josh to low-birthweight, physical, neurological, cognitive, and learning deficits. Baby Josh, whose mother denied him access to his paternal grandmother, the only person who wanted him, and who could care for him, who was neglected and emotionally abused by his mother, ignored by the Columbus County DSS, who should have intervened on his behalf to prevent his mother from abusing/neglecting him as she had done his other four siblings. Baby Josh who was torched by his mother while he slept in his crib, who would was denied his day in court, albeit posthumously, by the State of North Carolina, and the District Attorney of Columbus County, and whose murder has gone unpunished because the citizens of Columbus County, North Carolina, the United States and the World didn't give damn.

A little grave dug in sand – a wooden white cross etched with the name "Josh Cade Hinson," reminds us that Baby Josh, conceived in deception, born only to profit his mother, never feeling wanted or loved, murdered in his crib by the mother who put him there purportedly to sleep and not to die, -- a victim in life of the insufferable cruelty by his mother's rejection and neglect, now, even in death, he continues to be a victim of justice's abandonment because no one cared enough, or had the courage to step forward, to give Baby Josh his day in court.

A mom's perfect murder indeed!

Epilogue

How does one explain a mother murdering her own child, or, as Susan Smith's husband titled his book, *Beyond All Reason,* how could David Smith come to understand how his wife could buckle their two boys, Alex and Michael, into their car seats and then push the car into John D. Long Lake? He couldn't. He didn't. Her behavior would never make any sense. It was too bizarre. This was his wife. The woman he had loved! The mother of his two sons!

A mother killing her own child contradicts the dictum etched into the very cornerstone of human civilization: "A mother will risk her own life to save her offspring."

Not only our species but across almost all species, mothers die defending their young. And, even those species in which the mother may flee the predator, leaving her offspring behind, can be explained as necessary to propagate the species. But, kill her own? Never.

London-1888. "Jack the Ripper" disembowels his victims, spreading terror across two continents. Jeffrey Dahmer refrigerates body parts of young men so that he can cannibalize them as snacks, Hitler orders the gassing of 8 million Jews, Pol Pot, kills millions in the killing fields of Cambodia, thereby defying our definition of "being human," still when a mother murders her child, the very familial basis of human society trembles in torment doubt about its existence.

We label "Jack the Ripper" a "madman," Hitler, a monster, and Jeffrey Dahmer a "psychotic killer, "but we are

so emotionally paralyzed by a mother who murders her own
children that we have no word in our language to describe
this most incredulous of crimes.

In his proposed book, *Moms Who Murder Their
Children,* Dr. Coleman calls such behavior "pro-genocide."

So, what's in a name?

Springfield, Oregon. May 19, 1983. Diane Downs
shoots and kills her 7-year-old daughter Cheryl, and shoots,
intending to kill, her 3-year-old son Danny and 8-year-old
Christie. Arriving at the Emergency Room, where Cheryl is
DOA, the very pregnant mother yells, "Call the cops! He shot
my kids." An APB is put out for a shaggy-haired stranger,"
who had been standing in the road looking as if he needed
help. When the mother stops to help, the stranger demands
her car keys, and then "reached in and shoots my kids!"

She lied. Diane Downs was given a life sentence for
murder and attempted murder.

Peoria, Illinois. Firefighters picking their way through
smoldering ruins of Dr. Green's mini-mansion, discover the
body of her 14-year-old son in his bedroom and her 10-year-
old daughter in her bedroom – both trapped by a fatal fire.
The third child managed to crawl out on the garage and jump.
(Dr. Green holds out her arms to catch her daughter but pulls
them back when her daughter jumps.)

Arson experts determined the fire had been set with an
accelerant at the foot of the stairway so as to trap the children
in their upstairs bedrooms. (Dr. Green had been downstairs)

Certainly, Dr. Green, loving mother and physician
would never burn her own children to death!

Yes, she would, and did! Dr. Green, confronted with
the evidence, plea-bargained a life sentence instead of the
death penalty for two counts of murder one, and one count of
attempted murder. (She also faced another attempted murder
charge for having poisoned her husband.)

According to Greek mythology, Medea, sorceress and

daughter of Aeetes, guardian of the Golden Fleece, became so determined to win Jason's affection, she destroyed everyone who impeded his quest of the Fleece, including the killing of her own brother. Medea and Jason soon fled to Corinth where they settled and had two children. However, Jason's gaze soon fell upon the daughter of the king of Corinth. Medea enraged by Jason's betrayal, murdered her two children. "So, the children he had by me, he'll never see again."

In Euripides' play, Medea's nurse comments, "She hates her children...does not enjoy seeing them. I'm afraid she may be planning something rash. Her mind is dangerous. She will not endure mistreatment. I know this woman and fear her."

Some 2,500 years later, and much closer to home, Terri Hinson's friends, neighbors, and ex-husbands, and fathers of her five children were saying the same of her. Her own mother reported Terri to Columbus County Social Services for abandoning her three children to run off to Charlotte with her boyfriend. Her husband at the time reported that Terri would frequently leave the children alone while he was at work, so she could "run around." Neighbors reported seeing the children playing near the road and having to go out and rescue them from being hit by a car. Terri had been charged with neglect and should have had her children removed and her tubes tied years ago.

Terri Hinson signed the papers placing her first three children up for adoption, then later told law enforcement investigating the fire which killed baby Josh, that DSS had taken her children while she was in Charlotte looking for a job. Police had also been called because she'd left baby Josh alone in the car in the college parking lot.

Her closest friend reported that Terri Hinson would put Josh and Brittany to bed at 7:00 PM, "to get them out of the way." When Josh was about four months old, Terri instructed another close friend, "Don't rock him (Josh), don't

231

you pick him up, and don't talk to him." "I never saw her rock him, cuddle him, or sing to him."

A week before Josh died in the fire, Terri had tried to persuade her best friend to "take Brittany and Josh (adopt) them, if not both of them, then Josh."

Union, South Carolina, October 25, 1994. Susan Smith pounds on the door of Shirley and Rick McCloud screaming, "A black man has taken my kids and my car. I was at a red light. The black man put a gun to my head and told me to drive or he'd kill me. After driving around for miles, he ordered me out, saying he didn't have time to get them out of their car seats!"

No black man was ever found. What was found was the bodies of little Alex Smith, age 14 months and Michael Smith, age 3, strapped in their car seats in their mother's upside down Mazda at the bottom of John D. Long Lake.

Alex and Michael's mother, confronted with a failed lie detector test (Terri Hinson had failed hers, too – telling friends, "I was nervous.") and other evidence, confessed that she had pushed her car down the ramp into the lake drowning her two sons.

Why? Because the man of her dreams, who coincidently happened to be the rich son of the wealthiest man in Union, South Carolina, had told her he had no interest in continuing their affair because she had two children.

The choice: The rich boyfriend, or her sons Alex and Michael? Her sons would have to go.

Diane Downs's boyfriend viewed her three kids as too much baggage to continue this affair with a possessive female. There were others out there for the plucking who had no kids. Diane Downs pleaded that he accept the "total package." He balked. She piled her children into the car. Out of sight, she pulled off the road, turned around and shot her children, Cheryl, Danny, and Christie.

Terri Hinson tricked the well-off Kenneth Bryant into

getting her pregnant, ("I've just had kidney surgery and can't have any more children"). Once bearing his child, Terri could assert her rights to the front door of the Big House. However, when Mr. Bryant discovered he'd been flimflammed, he took off. Terry was stuck with a child she no longer needed nor ever wanted. What to do? Abortion? Well, not so long as there was a chance to extort money from Josh's grandmother.

Then, she met Rodney Strickland, who offered Terri a second chance to walk down easy street. Rodney had sustained a back injury from a fall at a construction site. Terry fondled the future Workmen's Comp settlement in her brain.

Terri needed a plan. First, she must replace Rodney's wife. No problem. Sex had always worked before. An affair, something she was certain Rodney had never experienced, should jump-start the "alienation of affection" process.

With years of experience, Terry seduced Rodney into moving from his wife's bed to hers. Not one to give something absent *quid pro quo*, Terri insisted Rodney pay the rent.

Not so fast. Rodney's wife filed a Complaint alleging Rodney, "without provocation, removed himself from the marital home on or about the 1st day of March, 1996... that the Plaintiff has and at all times been a faithful and dutiful spouse to the Defendant and has contributed her time, energies and efforts in establishing a home for the family... that upon information and belief, the Defendant is currently residing in Apartment 203 at Tabor Villa Apartments in Tabor City, North Carolina with another female to whom he is not married and is currently involved in an adulterous relationship with this female... that the Plaintiff be awarded custody of minor child... be granted a Divorce... the Defendant be ordered to pay child support... the Plaintiff be granted equitable distribution of all marital assets... and awarded alimony, both *pendente lite* and permanent."

Like a cornered cat, Terry attacked. In the answer to

the complaint, which Rodney signed, but Terry admitted drafting, Terry alleged that Rodney's wife, "went out 2-5 days each week to clubs... for the past eight years we" (Rodney and his wife) "shared about two nights a week as a family... seventy-five percent of that time was spent with the Plaintiff arguing over trivial matters. For approximately four years, the Plaintiff complained of headaches and refused sex... the Defendant and the female mentioned (in the Complaint) attend classes at Southeastern Community College and frequently study, along with others, at her home. This is easier since the female has two small children. The Defendant has been living with a couple since leaving the marital home. Dana Meares and Rocky Hammond." (When later asked, Dana's mother with whom Dana actually lives, stated Rodney has "never stayed at their house; not a single day!")

Mission accomplished. Terry could smell that Workman's Comp Settlement check.

The smell turned from flowers to rotting flesh when Rodney announced in the presence of their friends, "I've already raised two young-uns, and I ain't about to be raisin' two more, especially when they already got daddy's who should be paying child support like I gotta do."

Terry winced; Rodney's edict blew her future out of the water.
Brittany and Josh had to go. No problem a little house fire couldn't solve.

Dr. Green and Medea present a slightly different variation on Dr. Coleman's pro-genocide theme. Rather than murdering their children to appease a balking boyfriend, Dr. Green and Medea killed their children to avenge their husband's affairs, Medea asserting, "So the children he had by me, he'll never see again." For her part, Dr. Green, who had been unsuccessfully poisoning her husband for many months, finally decided incinerating her three children would work where the poison had failed.

Despite the slightly different twist in the Green and Medea instances of pro genocide, in all these cases, the children of these mothers became expendable.

Instead, as is the rule that children come first, these mothers had reversed the rule to read, "The male relationship comes first – even if it means killing one's own children."

In the Downs, Smith, and Hinson examples, boyfriends affirmed, "It's either me or your kids. Your choice." The mothers choose the boyfriend.

With Medea and Dr. Green, their vengeful murder of their own children when their husband's gaze wandered, suggests that for these women too, children were merely a means to securing their relationship in the first place – children were a means to an end – a weapon. Consequently, when Medea and Dr. Green realized their relationship war had been lost, after all, they used the same weapons they had deployed to conquer the male, to now destroy him.

Still, the point to be made is that for all these mothers, children were tools, weapons, a ploy to control an adult male, to force a relationship into existence, because the essential "bonding" that normally occurs among other females is not available to these mothers.

In "*Moms Who Murder Their Children,*" Dr. Coleman explains that these mothers never bonded with their children, because as children themselves, they never bonded with their parents. As a result, they feel adrift, precluded from that sense of belonging, desperate, panicked to have, and hold onto, someone. They must substitute control for bonding, jumping from one relationship to the next, lying, threatening suicide, frantic sex, desperate, immaculate conceptions – whatever it takes, to create the illusion of bonding.

The oldest of five children born to a harsh Bible-pounding father and a weak, submissive mother, Diane Downs was precluded from being "Daddy's Little Girl," or

Mommy's Little Helper." Alone, unwanted, and estranged even from her siblings, Diane would later report feeling like "The Ugly Duckling." All that changed for the worse, when at age 12, her father is alleged to have begun sexually assaulting and molesting her. Diane learned to use her wits and her sexuality to control people, i.e., MAKE teachers pay attention to her by getting all A's and to MAKE men want her by flaunting her sexuality. Babies and stormy affairs followed, but no love, Thus, Diane Downs was incapable of giving or receiving love, forcing her to become increasingly desperate with each failed relationship. Only able to control and manipulate men, thereby dooming herself, she finally shot her three children riding helplessly in the back seat of her car, in order to HAVE a man – someone – anyone.

Susan Smith, never bonding with her parents, and alleging having been sexually molested by her step-father, learned that sexual attractiveness could be used to control and manipulate men – that sex could substitute for love. The trouble was that sex produced babies, who, should they fail to deliver a sense of belonging, could also slam the door to future relationships. Faced with the horror of staying in a relationship which had already failed to deliver its promise of a sense of belonging, or being free to run into the arms of her new hope, Susan Smith chose to drown her two sons.

Terri Hinson, the daughter of a severe, abusive and assaultive father and a steely cold, assaultive, and erratic mother, and who may have been raped by her brother, jumps from bed to bed, using sex and having babies as a way to control and manipulate men. Terri's friends upon visiting Terri's house would report that they never observed any signs of love – no hugging, no "warm fuzzies," no signs of endearment between Terri and her mother and between Terri and her children. Terri herself would report she and her mother never "got along." Indeed, Terri's mother reported that Terri stole $1,800 dollars from her mother when she ran

236

off to Charlotte with her boyfriend, abandoning her three children and her husband. Terri would soon put these three children up for adoption. They were getting in the way of her quest to hold onto her boyfriend at the time. When Brittany and Josh kept Rodney from saying "yes" to marrying Terri, she torched their bedrooms, just as Dr. Green had done.

Dr. Leon Leifer, assistant clinical professor of psychiatry at Columbia Medical School, of Physicians and Surgeons and a leading expert on parents who murder their children, describes the Susan Smiths of the world as a sub-type of Borderline Personality, Dr. Leifer calls "impulse-control disorder," in which the person, usually female, takes drastic means to get what she wants and, in the process, demonstrates a commensurate lack of empathy for those who get in her way.

Dr. Coleman, who has both personal and professional experience with mothers who have abandoned and/or murdered their children, concurs that these moms are not sub-types, but rather, full-blown Borderline Personality Disorders, defined by DSM-IV as having "unstable/intense possessive relationships, are compulsive in their frantic efforts to heal real or imagined estrangement, are impulsive, compulsive liars, are promiscuous, drug abusers, make repeated suicidal threats, manifest erratic behavior, paranoia, and mood instability, as well as being volatile, physically and verbally abusive, and, as the name implies, may, from time to time, cross the line into transient psychosis.

However, rather than being an exotic Borderline subtype, Dr. Coleman believes that moms who murder their children are on a continuum of all Borderline mothers, all of whom suffer from the basic inability to bond, therefore unable to nurture, and certainly incapable of putting their children's needs and wants ahead of their own desperate to control.

Whereas a few abandon their children, while a very few, murder theirs, for Dr. Coleman, as with the male psychopath, the essential symptom is an inability to bond, first with their parents, and ultimately with their own mates, children, or friends. They must, therefore, substitute control and manipulation as a self-delusion of a loving relationship.

The only good news is that moms who murder their children can be predicted from that pool of birth to 6-year-old girls who, for a variety of observable reasons, i.e., paternal abuse, incest, maternal weakness, submissiveness, or meanness, will be precluded from bonding. with either parent. They will be possessive, controlling, and manipulative in all their relationships in school, will have no lasting friendships, and will seek out the weak, meek, and wounded to dominate.

In fact, vigilant teachers and a Columbus County Department of Social Services could have seen Terri Hinson's inevitable becoming a murderous mom, if not from the callous indifference and lack of nurturing shown her first three children, then, the reports by neighbors of her constant neglect, and if missing all those signs, certainly the act of signing papers to have her three children adopted, should have been a red flag.

The tragedy of tragedies, Baby Josh's death could have been prevented. Failing that, the least we can do is review our mistakes – our failure to read the signposts – as a minimum, appoint a guardian *ad litem* for each infant born to mothers, who like Terri Hinson, have demonstrated an unwillingness and/or inability to care and nurture their children, and consider that, if said mom neglects, abandons, or abuses a child, and insists on receiving State support, that support will be contingent upon future infertility.

Meanwhile, despite the defensiveness anticipated from the State and County criminal justice system and the media, who failed Josh the first time, we must, because it is the right thing to do, petition the Attorney General of State of North Carolina to grant Josh Cade Hinson the justice, once denied.

Justice for Baby Josh

There is no Statute of Limitation for First Degree Murder.

Petition

I/We _____,
of _____
address, having read this book and considered the evidence
presented therein, do hereby petition the Attorney General of
the State of North Carolina, and any and all other authorities
with jurisdiction in the death of Josh Cade Hinson, in
Columbus County, North Carolina, on October 20, 1996, to
re-open the case based on the new evidence contained herein,
alleging Josh Cade Hinson, was the victim of murder by
arson at the hands of his mother, Terry Louise Hinson, aka
Terry Louise Strickland, posthumously.

Date _____

Signed _____